Subject
and Predicate
in Logic and
Grammar

By the same author

Introduction to Logical Theory
Individuals
The Bounds of Sense
Logico-Linguistic Papers
Freedom and Resentment and other essays

Subject and Predicate in Logic and Grammar

P. F. Strawson

Methuen & Co Ltd

First published in 1974
by Methuen & Co Ltd
11 New Fetter Lane, London EC4P 4EE
Reprinted 1976
© 1974 P. F. Strawson

Printed in Great Britain
at the
University Printing House, Cambridge
(Harry Myers, University Printer)

ISBN 0 416 82190 1 (hardback)
ISBN 0 416 82200 2 (paperback)

564316
H

Distributed in the USA by
HARPER & ROW PUBLISHERS, INC.
BARNES & NOBLE IMPORT DIVISION

Contents

Preface vii

Part One: The Subject in Logic

CHAPTER ONE: THE 'BASIC
COMBINATION' 3

1. Some formal differences 4
2. Spatio-temporal particulars and general
   concepts 13
3. Propositional combination: a tripartition of
   function 20
4. Formal differences explained for the basic case 22
5. The generalization of the form 35
6. An objection answered 37

CHAPTER TWO: PROPER NAMES—AND
OTHERS 41

1. What is the use of them? 42
2. Names and identity 51
3. Names in the framework of logic: proper
   names, variable names and descriptive names 57
4. General names 66

Part Two: The Subject in General

CHAPTER THREE: LANGUAGE-TYPES AND PERSPICUOUS GRAMMARS 75

1. Essential grammar and variable grammar 75
2. Language-Types 1 and 2 80
3. Language-Type 3: relations 84
4. Further minor enrichments: space–time indication 94

CHAPTER FOUR: SUBSTANTIATION AND ITS MODES 99

1. Special case and general function 99
2. Some supporting evidence 104
3. Modes of substantiation 110
4. Further matters: existence; negation; scope 113

CHAPTER FIVE: THE GENERALIZATION OF THE SUBJECT 120

1. Derivative roles and derivative elements 120
2. The generalization of the subject 125
3. The fitting in of features 135
4. Further questions 138
   Index 140

Preface

That singular predication lies at the core of logic, and that the fundamental cases of singular predication are those in which the designated individuals are spatio–temporal particulars or, more specifically, substantial occupants of space with some endurance through time—these are neither of them thoughts of any great originality. Yet these thoughts may still yield gains in understanding, both in logic and in general grammar. They may help us to trace some formal characteristics of logic and its grammar to their roots in general features of thought and experience; and they may help us also to observe how the grammatical structures of a large group of non-formalized languages, though rooted in these same features, may naturally develop, in various ways, along other lines. These, at any rate, are two of the things attempted in the present essay.

Logic, though it may dazzle us with the clarity of its structures, forms only one part—the first—of that modern *trivium* which now deservedly holds as central a place in liberal studies as ever its predecessor did. The other parts are general syntax-semantics and what, for want of a better word, may be called pragmatics. There is no reason why that dazzling first part, as we have it, should dictate the course of the second, and clearly no possibility of its dictating the course of the third. Rather, for full, or philosophical, comprehension, all three should be held, and viewed, in relation to each other and to investigations variously shared by, or apportioned between, metaphysics, epistemology and philosophy of mind. Some further illustration of these general convictions will be found in the chapters that follow; e.g. in the bringing together of the first and third parts of the modern *trivium* in the second chapter; and at many points in Part Two. But the book is an essay, not a treatise, still less a technical treatise; and I have nowhere aimed at formal precision.

The material on which the book is based has been used in seminars in Oxford and in Princeton; and its second part formed the substance of a series of lectures delivered at Irvine in 1971 and, in a shortened form, at University College, London, in 1973. I am deeply indebted to my critics, students and colleagues alike, at all these places; and in particular to Professors Gilbert Harman and Richard Grandy, at Princeton.

The discussion of *term-ordering*, on pp. 86–93, is to appear in *Crítica* in 1974; I am grateful to the editor and publishers of that journal for permission to reproduce it here. Finally, I should like to thank Mrs. E. Hinkes for typing the book.

P.F.S.
Oxford
September 1973

Part
One

The
Subject
in Logic

I
The
'Basic
Combination'

It is a commonplace that a certain kind of combination—which we call 'predication'—has a fundamental position in our current logic. We write down the schemata 'Fx', 'Fxy', '$Fxyz$', etc.; and what we thus represent are the general forms of unquantified and uncompounded proposition which our logic recognizes. We can obtain sentences exemplifying these forms by replacing the 'x's, 'y's, 'F's, etc., by appropriate terms or expressions, which may themselves be unstructured or simple. The results of such replacements are complete sentences. In the austerer logical language favoured by Quine, which allows no singular terms but variables, this method of obtaining complete sentences from our schemata is not available. Instead, to obtain a sentence capable of expressing a proposition, of saying something true or false, we should have to introduce quantifiers, binding the variables. Whatever the merits of this austerity, it would seem that we shall keep our logical closer to our natural language by allowing complete sentences not to involve quantification.

It is not, of course, a random feature of these schemata that in writing them we employ two different sorts of symbol, viz. the lower-case 'x's and '*y*'s on the one hand, the upper case '*F*'s and '*G*'s on the other; individual variables, as we are accustomed to saying, on the one hand, predicate-letters on the other, though in the context of the present discussion the former are perhaps better called name-letters. In writing the schemata, then, thinking of them, as I suggested, as forms exemplified by complete sentences, it seems at least that we are representing a certain kind of union either of two different sorts of expression (or term) or, at least, of expressions (or terms) with two different kinds of role. We have names for the two different sorts of expression or of expression-in-a-role. We may speak of 'designators' or 'definite singular terms' or 'names' or 'logical-subject-expressions' or 'subject-terms' on the one hand; of 'predicate-expressions' or 'predicate-terms' on the other. I shall often speak simply of *subjects* and *predicates*, treating these titles as correlative, as standing for expressions-in-a-role.

My first aim is to try to explain the general nature of this duality of role, the general relative nature, that is, of the terms combined in this basic combination of predication. It seems that this must be a question of some importance. If current logic has the significance which we are inclined to attach to it, and which our contemporary style of philosophizing in particular assumes, then it must reflect fundamental features of our thought about the world. And at the core of logic lie the structures here in question, the 'basic combination' (as Quine once called it) of predication.

What, then, distinguishes subject-terms from predicate-terms? I begin with some formal differences, or alleged differences, which call for explanation rather than themselves constituting an explanation of the distinction.

1. Some formal differences

I. PREDICATE-TERMS ARE FORMALLY RESTRICTED IN A WAY IN WHICH SUBJECT-TERMS ARE NOT

One distinction is immediately suggested by the schemata we have before us. Sentences exemplifying those schemata may contain more than one subject-term but only one predicate-term. So subject-terms are distinguished from predicate-terms by the fact that more than one of them may appear in some forms of such sentences. Our knowledge of the grammar or syntax of our logical languages enables us to say more than this. Any term functioning as a predicate-term is restricted, as regards its appearance in a complete sentence, to just one of the listed forms: it is restricted *either* to a form with just one place for a subject-term *or* to a form with just two places *or* to a form with just three . . . and so on. But no subject-term is so restricted. One and the same subject-term may appear in a form with any number of subject-places.

Russell, at one time, held that the terms of certain sentences of these forms—those sentences which resisted any further analysis—stood for or specified extra-linguistic items of two different types, namely individuals and universals, items which could be said to be constituents of, or to occur in, the atomic propositions expressed by such sentences. Individuals were defined by him as items which could occur in atomic propositions with any number of constituent elements; whereas a universal could occur only in a proposition with an appropriate fixed number of constituent elements. These definitions reflect, and are intended to reflect, the formal distinction just drawn between subject-terms and predicate-terms. They could not be held to explain that distinction unless, at least, some independent account were given of the nature of the extra-linguistic items concerned. Russell's procedure obviously involved a fairly strong assumption about the nature of sentences expressing atomic propositions: viz. the assumption that an extra-linguistic item specified by a subject-term in one such sentence could never be specified by a predicate-term in another, or vice versa. But when we think of such sentences as 'John is black' or 'That door is green' on the one hand and 'Black is beautiful' or 'Green is a soothing colour' on the other, we must again wonder both about the nature of the extra-linguistic items concerned and about the criteria of atomicity in propositions.

Let us leave the Russellian metaphysics of atomic propositions on one side. What we have so far is a distinction between predicate-terms and subject-terms which is a formal, and specifically a grammatical or syntactical, distinction. As regards their appearance in complete sentences predicate-terms are restricted in ways in which subject-terms are not. We can scarcely, however, regard this as explaining the general nature of the distinction for us. Rather, we may hope to have it explained by whatever explains the general nature of the kind of combination in question.

2. COMPOUND AND NEGATIVE PREDICATE-TERMS

Now for another distinction which is also formal but not purely syntactical. For its exposition we must introduce the propositional connectives and certain analogues of these, which we will call, neutrally for the moment, term-connectives. We may express the distinction as follows. We can coherently enrich our logic with what we may call negative and compound (e.g. disjunctive or conjunctive) predicate-terms, but there is no strictly parallel way in which we can coherently enrich our logic with negative or compound subject-terms. Thus suppose we have a simple subject-predicate sentence, 'Fa'. We form its contradictory or negation, '$-(Fa)$'. Now we introduce term-negation for the predicate-term, 'F', forming the negative term, '$\overline{F}$', which enters into the predicative combination with 'a' to form the sentence, '$\overline{F}a$', in which 'a' is subject and '$\overline{F}$' a new style of predicate, viz. a negative predicate. Then '$-(Fa)$' is logically equivalent to '$\overline{F}a$'. Similarly, given a conjunction of two simple subject–predicate sentences with the same subject and different predicates, say '(Fa) and (Ga)', we can introduce the conjunctive predicate of those two predicates and form an equivalent sentence, '$(F$ and $G)a$', in which the compound term, 'F and G', enters into predicative combination with the subject, 'a'. Similarly, again, we have as equivalent to the disjunctive sentence, '(Fa) or (Ga)', the uncompounded sentence, '$(F$ or $G)a$', which includes a compound, disjunctive predicate.

In general, we can negate and compound monadic predicates in a style exactly analogous to that in which we can negate and compound propositions and the internal logic of predicate-composition is exactly analogous to that of propositional logic. For example just as '$-(p \,\&\, q)$' and '$-p \vee -q$' are proposition-equivalent, so '$\overline{F \text{ and } G}$' and '$\overline{F}$ or $\overline{G}$' are predicate-equivalent, i.e. any proposition of the form '$\overline{(F \text{ and } G)}a$' is equivalent to any proposition of the form '$(\overline{F}$ or $\overline{G})a$'.

Granted that we can enrich our logic with compound and negative predicates, it is easy to show that we cannot coherently frame compound and negative subject-terms in a symmetrical fashion. For suppose we have the following sentence, a disjunction of conjunctions:

(1) (Fa and Ga) or (Fb and Gb).

Then, by the rule permitting conjunctive predicates, (1) is equivalent to

(2) (F and G)a or (F and G)b.

But if we can frame compound (in this case disjunctive) names, then (2) is equivalent to

(3) (F and G)(a or b)

and (3) can be expanded into

6

(4) $F(a$ or $b)$ and $G(a$ or $b)$

which is in its turn equivalent to

(5) $(Fa$ or $Fb)$ and $(Ga$ or $Gb)$.

But (5) is equivalent to (1) only if

(6) $((p \,\&\, q) \vee (r \,\&\, s)) \equiv ((p \vee r) \,\&\, (q \vee s))$

is a valid formula. But (6) is not a valid formula. A parallel argument will discredit conjunctive names.

As for negative names, suppose we have the following conjunctive sentence:

(1) Fa and Ga.

Then, by double negation, this is equivalent to

(2) $-(-(Fa$ and $Ga))$

which, by the introduction of a conjunctive predicate, is equivalent to

(3) $-(-((F$ and $G)a))$.

If we can frame negative subjects, (3) is equivalent to

(4) $-((F$ and $G)\bar{a})$

and (4) can be expanded into

(5) $-(\overline{Fa}$ and $\overline{Ga})$

which will be equivalent to

(6) $-(-(Fa)$ and $-(Ga))$.

Now (6) is equivalent to

(7) Fa or Ga.

But evidently (1) is not equivalent to (7)

Such formal arguments do nothing to explain, or even to confirm, the doctrine that our logic can be enriched with negative and compound predicates, but not with negative and compound subjects. They show that there cannot be *both* negative and compound subjects *and* negative and compound predicates; but, by themselves, the arguments give no reason for admitting the latter and disallowing the former rather than admitting the former and disallowing the latter.[1] They leave us without either an explanation of the doctrine's truth or a reason for accepting

[1] See R. H. Grimm, 'Names and predicables', *Analysis*, vol. 26, 1965–6.

it as true. Later, we shall find both at once. For the moment, let us accept the doctrine without either reason or explanation.

Accepting the doctrine, and bringing it to bear on certain constructions we find in natural language, we may note the need for a distinction between a truly compound term and a merely apparent compounding of terms which, from the logical point of view, simply abbreviates a compound sentence and yields no genuine term. Suppose we unadventurously hypothesize that 'Tom' and 'William' may, in English, serve as subject-terms and 'rides', 'drinks', 'is lying', 'is mad' as predicate-terms. When, then, we are faced with such a sentence as

> Either Tom or William both rides and drinks

the formal argument alone is sufficient to force us to deny the status of genuine compound term to at least one of the pair of expressions, 'Either Tom or William' and 'both rides and drinks'; and our acceptance of the doctrine of compound predicate-terms encourages us to award this status to 'both rides and drinks'. And English bears us out. For, as far as natural English goes, we can argue validly from

> Either Tom or William both rides and drinks

to

> Either Tom both rides and drinks or William both rides and drinks

and vice versa; but we cannot argue validly from

> Either Tom or William both rides and drinks

to

> Either Tom or William rides and either Tom or William drinks

and vice versa.

The second pair of transformations is inadmissible, while the first pair of transformations is admissible. This is precisely what we should expect if 'both rides and drinks' is a genuine compound term.

It would be a mistake, however, to jump to the conclusion that all expressions which appear to be formally similar to 'both rides and drinks' can safely be counted as genuine compound terms. For example, the sentence

> Both Tom and William are either mad or lying

is ambiguous. The interpretation which makes it equivalent to

8

> Either both Tom and William are mad or both Tom and William are lying

is at least as natural as the interpretation which makes it equivalent to

> Tom is either mad or lying and William is either mad or lying.

On the second interpretation we can indeed count 'either mad or lying' as a genuine compound term. But if we adopt the first interpretation, we must reject the claim of 'either mad or lying' to be a genuine compound term, and say that the sentence, so interpreted, contains no such term.

The formal difference between subjects and predicates which we here formally accept is surely a very striking difference. It has been remarked on more than once in the remote and recent history of the subject.[2] Regarded in its purely formal aspect, however, the difference cannot be regarded as explaining for us the general nature of the distinction and combination of subject and predicate. Rather, it awaits a justifying explanation.

3. 'THE PREDICATE IS "TRUE OF" (OR "FALSE OF") WHAT THE SUBJECT STANDS FOR'

It is sometimes implied or suggested, rather than directly stated, that the phrase 'true of' (or 'false of') supplies a clue to the distinction and relation, of subject and predicate. The idea seems to be, roughly, that taking a subject–predicate proposition to be true (or false) is the same thing as taking the predicate to be true (or false) of what the subject stands for; but not conversely. This cannot be more than a rough expression of the idea. Suppose 'Socrates swims' is a subject-predicate sentence, with 'Socrates' as subject and 'swims' as predicate. No one at all fastidious would allow ' "swims" is true of Socrates' as tolerable English. However, the following is perfectly allowable:

> It is true of Socrates that he swims

as is also

> It is true of Socrates that Socrates swims.

---

[2] Notably, as regards negation, by P. T. Geach. See *Reference and Generality*, Ithaca, Cornell Univ. Press, 1969, p. 32; *Logic Matters*, Oxford, Blackwell, 1973, pp. 45, 70; and elsewhere. The formal argument regarding 'negative subjects' on p. 7 above is adapted from an argument of Geach's in *Reference and Generality*.

Similarly 'John beats Mary' admits of the following paraphrases:

> It is true of (the couple), John and Mary, that John beats Mary
> It is true of (the couple), John and Mary, that the former beats the latter

and again of the following

> It is true of John that John (*or* he) beats Mary
> It is true of Mary that John beats Mary (*or* her).

So the doctrine can presumably be understood as the doctrine that this form of paraphrase is always admissible for subject-predicate sentences, so long as subjects and predicates preserve the positions just illustrated in the paraphrases; but they cannot exchange their positions.

To the doctrine as stated it may be objected that the following sentences are also perfectly admissible, though unusual, English and hence equally allowable as paraphrases:

> It is true of *swimming* that Socrates swims
> It is true of *swimming* that Socrates does it

and

> It is true of *beating* that John beats Mary
> It is true of *beating* that John does it to Mary.

No distinction between subject and predicate is therefore marked by the availability of paraphrase in the 'true of' construction.

The reply to this objection is presumably to invoke a requirement, not so far explicitly stated, on the procedure of paraphrase: the requirement that (apart from the permitted replacement, in the embedded that-clause, of noun or noun-phrase by pronoun, or verb or verb-phrase by proverb) no change is to be allowed in the grammatical form or category of the expressions which figure in the original subject–predicate sentence. They are simply to be slotted in to the scheme

$$\text{It is true of } x \text{ that } \begin{cases} x\,y \\ y\,x \end{cases}$$

as they stand, with merely the freedom of pro-nominal or pro-verbal substitution at the second 'x'.

Now as a matter of grammar the phrase 'is true of' requires to be followed by a noun or noun-phrase; and a noun or noun-phrase (or pronoun) requires complementing by a verb or verb-phrase to form a clause. So, with the addition of the requirement needed to block the objection, the distinction which was to be drawn with the help of the phrase 'true of' reduces to the purely grammatical point that in a subject–predicate sentence in English, the subject is a noun or noun-phrase and the predicate a verb or verb-phrase.

To say that the point is purely grammatical is not, of course, to say that it is unimportant, even for the present phase of our inquiry, let alone for the inquiry as a whole. What is it, we may now ask, about the logical status of predicate and the grammatical form of the verb which make them apt for each other? But it will be seen that our distinction in terms of the phrase 'true of' has led us to further questions rather than to answers to our original question: and also that the phrase 'true of' itself, with whatever peculiar promise of illumination it may have held out, has disappeared from view behind the grammatical distinction which replaces it.

Still we may be aware of some vague suggestiveness in the idea that it is peculiarly the function of expressions in the predicate-role to yield truth or falsity when attached to expressions in the subject-role, and not the other way about; and aware, too, of a connection between this thought and the fact that the predicate has, in English, the form of the verb; and of a connection, also, with the fact, just remarked on, that we can obtain the negation of a subject–predicate sentence by replacing the predicate-term by its own negation, whereas we can do no such thing with the subject term. But all this demands, rather than constitutes, explanation.

4. 'SUBJECT-TERMS, BUT NOT PREDICATE-TERMS, ARE ADMISSIBLE IN PLACES WHERE VARIABLES OF QUANTIFICATION ARE ADMISSIBLE'

Next I mention a further alleged difference between subject-terms and predicates. The principal exponent of this alleged difference, viz. Quine, claims for it, indeed, not only that it is *a* difference between subject- and predicate-terms, but that it is the *only* difference. This last claim, at least, may seem surprising in view of what has gone before. Have we not already mentioned differences? But let us see what the difference is said to consist in.

In *Ontological Relativity* Quine says: '. . . the mark of a name (subject-term) is its admissibility in positions of variables'.[3] In *The*

---

[3] *Ontological Relativity and Other Essays*, New York, Columbia Univ. Press, 1970, p. 62.

Philosophy of Logic he says: 'What distinguishes a name is that it can stand coherently in the place of a variable, in predication . . . Predicates are not names; predicates are the other parties in predication.'[4] In 'Existence and Quantification' he says, more fully: 'When we schematize a sentence in the predicative way "*Fa*" or "*a* is an *F*", our recognition of an "*a*" part and an "*F*" part turns strictly on our use of variables of quantification; the "*a*" represents a part of the sentence that stands where a quantifiable variable could stand, and the "*F*" represents the rest.'[5] There are two parties, then, to a complete, unquantified predication, a subject-part and a predicate-part. What distinguishes them is nothing other than the fact that the subject-part can coherently yield its place to a variable of quantification and the predicate-part cannot. If quantification should lapse, or be dispensed with, the distinction of subject and predicate would lapse with it.

The doctrine that names can, and predicates cannot, stand in positions accessible to variables of quantification can be, and has been, questioned. If it were merely a stipulated feature of the grammar of an artificial notation, there would be no point in questioning it and no need to defend it. It seems likely that Quine regards it as more than this. I shall not question it now, however: for there is another question to raise. Suppose we accepted this ground of distinction between subject and predicate terms. What reason could there be for presenting it as the *sole* ground of the distinction? This question again has interest only if such presentation is not merely an internal feature of the presentation of the grammar of a limited logical language. But again it seems likely that Quine regards it as more than this. We may get some light on his reasons by considering the character of that ideally austere language favoured by Quine in which subject-terms have no place at all. What in that language takes the place that would be theirs if they had a place, is a certain combination of existential quantifier, predicate and variables. Where, in a language with names, we have '*Fa*', in Quine's nameless language we have something like '($\exists x$) (uniquely-*A x* and *Fx*)'. Instead of 'Socrates swims' we have 'Something is uniquely Socratic and swims' or 'Something which is uniquely Socratic swims'. Instead of 'Socrates' *tout court* we have 'Something which is uniquely Socratic'. As far as this language is concerned, names (and subject-terms in general) are to be seen simply as *abbreviations* for such constructions as these. The basic construction which yields a complete sentence is the combination of

---

[4] *The Philosophy of Logic*, Englewood Cliffs, N.J., Prentice-Hall, 1970, pp. 27–8.
[5] *Ontological Relativity*, p. 95.

existential quantifier and bound variable with a predicate. A name (or subject-term) is distinctively characterized as an expression which can stand in the place of a bound variable because it simply abbreviates such a construction as has just been described, with an extra bound variable awaiting its predicate. A name can go in the place of a variable because a bound variable can go in the place of a variable.

It seems that, connectives apart, Quine regards existential quantification and predicates as supplying the bedrock of language or, at least, of any tolerably developed language. On this view, the simplest uncompounded sentence having a structure characteristic of a tolerably developed language is the result of combining existential quantifier and bound variable with a single predicate. Predicates simply are those items of vocabulary which thus combine with quantifiers to yield a sentence. Names, and subject-terms generally, are simply an inessential abbreviatory convenience, to be explained in the way indicated. *There is nothing else to be said about them than this.* And this is precisely the force of saying that the distinction between subjects and predicates 'turns strictly on our use of the variables of quantification'. We may think that the doctrine could have been less puzzlingly expounded. We cannot object to it as an account of the introduction of redundant, abbreviatory forms into an ideally simplified language. We have as yet no reason to accept it as an account of the actual role of subject-terms in natural language.

So much for the view that ability to stand in the place of variables is *the* mark which distinguishes subject-terms from predicate-terms. What of the view that it is at least *one* mark of this distinction, because there can be no quantifying into predicate-place? So much doctrine comes along with this view that I shall, for the time being, leave open the question of its truth, remarking simply that, if it is true, its truth calls also for explanation and, if false, the fact that it has seemed true demands no less.

2. Spatio–temporal particulars and general concepts

The general relative natures of the terms combined in the fundamental combination of predication—the differences or alleged differences between subjects and predicates—have so far been discussed in almost exclusively formal terms, in terms belonging to formal logic itself or to grammar. To understand the matter fully, we must be prepared to use a richer vocabulary, a range of notions which fall outside these formal limits. We assume that the subject–predicate duality, and hence the differences so far remarked on, reflect some fundamental features of our thought about the world. It is to the question, what those fundamental features are, that we must now turn.

That thought about the world involves general concepts is a truth, or platitude, which most philosophers accept, however much they may differ in the account they wish ultimately to give of it. It is a correlative truth, much insisted on by Kant, that the use of concepts, or their primary use, is in thought about the world, and, more specifically, in judgment, or the conscious framing or holding of beliefs, as to what is the case. Now the aim of judgment is truth; and a given judgment or belief is true just in so far as things are as one who holds that belief or makes that judgment thereby holds them to be. This is the platitude enshrined in anything which calls itself a Correspondence Theory of Truth. It is how things are in the world or in reality or in fact that determines whether our beliefs or judgments, and the propositions we affirm in expressing them, are true or false.

If we now ask how it is that we are able to make judgments, or form beliefs, about the reality, with a fair prospect of their being true, the philosophical tradition, or part of it, is again ready with a familiar answer. The answer is that we are made aware of the reality, in experience. It is experience of the world which fundamentally makes possible the use of concepts in judgment about it.

This answer is too weakly stated as it stands. Empiricism gives the screw an extra turn. (Here, when I speak of empiricism, I do not mean merely the classical, atomistic empiricism of Berkeley and Hume and their successors; I mean a strand in a tradition which, since Kant, embraces us all.) Experience is not to be conceived of as merely, as it were, a convenient link with the world, enabling the concept-user to go into action as a judgment-former with a fair prospect of forming true beliefs. The connection between judgment, concept and experience is closer than that. It is not, by itself, even enough to say, as Kant did, that concepts of the real are nothing at all to a potential user of them except in so far as they relate directly or indirectly to a possible experience of the real. More especially, as he also realized, those concepts which enter into our basic or least theoretical beliefs, into our fundamental judgments, are just those concepts which enter most intimately and immediately into our common experience of the world. They are what—special training apart— we *experience* the world *as* exemplifying, what we *see* things and situations *as* cases of. Correlatively, experience is awareness of the world as exemplifying *them*. We should not say that

14

judgments at this level are made on the basis of experience. Rather we should say that at this level judgment, concept and experience are merged; that seeing and believing really are, at this level, one. Of course this would be an exaggeration; for judgment may not only be corrected, it may be suspended; or assent may be denied, we may refuse to believe what our senses tell us. But it is only an exaggeration and a corrigible one. (It should be evident that the concepts I here speak of are not, in general, concepts of simple, sensory qualities, though they may include such.)

Now a general concept is general in this sense: it is capable, in principle, of being exemplified in any number of different particular cases. Our grasp of a general concept must include our grasp of this possibility or it is not a grasp of a general concept at all. If we take this point together with the previous point, we have the result that—if we are to have any use of any general concepts at all—it must be possible in principle for us to encounter in experience different particular cases and distinguish them as different while recognizing them as alike in being all cases falling under the same concept. The fulfilment of this requirement has, for us, a peculiarly intimate connection with the two great notions of Space and Time, of spatiality and temporality.

The connection is easily made. Surveying a spatial extent, we may distinguish, at the same moment, different particular instances of one general concept, as when we see at once two sheep in a field or two red triangles on a screen. Here spatial, not temporal, separation and relation are invoked: the simultaneous presence of two spatially distinct particular instances of the same concept. But we can as easily mention a case in which temporal, not spatial, separation is invoked: a succession, say, of high-pitched blasts from a policeman's whistle or of long and short signals from a Morse code transmitter. Or we can mix both cases together.

It might be asked why we should thus give a special place to the notions of Space and Time in connection with the notion of different particular instances of a general concept (and hence with the very notion of the generality of a concept). Will not different particular instances of a general concept normally be distinguished, and distinguishable in experience, by something else than the difference of spatial or temporal position? My car is indeed in a different position from your car; but it is also of a different colour, and is scratched in a manner peculiar to it. Did not Leibniz insist that every leaf could be seen to differ from every other if you looked hard enough? And even if this is not always so, is it not enough that it is usually or often so or that it could always be so?

The answer to this is very simple. Suppose it to be the case that every two leaves differ from each other in some respect other than the spatio–temporal; and so for other things. The fact remains that there would not *be two* leaves, thus to differ further, unless they differed spatio–temporally. There could not be two leaves which differed in some respect but which were spatio–temporally indistinguishable.

And now it might be said: It is true of course of concepts of *spatio-temporal* things that if two instances of one such concept differ at all, then they differ spatio–temporally. But might there not be general concepts such that we could encounter and distinguish *in experience* different particular instances of those concepts, and yet such that their instances were not spatio–temporal things at all? It is true that Kant found no contradiction in the thought of forms of sensible intuition other than the spatio–temporal. But I suggest that the thought, at best, leaves us quite blank. Having, for us, no empirical content, it is, as Kant himself might say, nothing to us. As far as we are concerned, the framework of experience is spatio–temporal, and the notion of different particular instances of a general concept, encounterable and distinguishable in experience, is linked to the notion of particular items distinguishable and relatable in the spatial and temporal terms of that framework.

Let us now consider the general relative natures of these items (spatio–temporal particulars) and of the general concepts they may exemplify. Such concepts, of course, are of vastly different sorts: there are concepts of relatively standing properties or qualities of particulars; of species or, more generally, kinds to which particulars may belong; of types of action or undergoing into which particulars may enter; of types of state or condition which they may be in. And these distinctions are crossed by another: the distinction between those concepts which are such that, in order to specify fully a particular case of the concept's application, a single particular-specification is required, and those concepts which are such that, in order to specify fully a particular case of the concept's application, more than one particular-specification is required. The latter we call relational concepts.

Particulars also are of many different sorts. We cannot distinguish and identify particulars just as such. We distinguish and identify them under concepts of kinds of particular. If we ask, absolutely in general, what distinguishes one particular of a given kind from another particular of that kind, we have the answer already before us. There may be two particulars of the same kind as like as you please in respect of the general concepts they exemplify. There is no logical limit to what can be shared by particulars in the way of general concepts. (This applies not only to single particulars, but to pairs or trios, etc., of related particulars.) But there is a logical limit to what particulars can share. They cannot both be of the same kind and share just the same tract of space–time.

Of course particulars of the same kind may *succeed* each other in the same space. And some kinds of particulars are such that one particular of the kind may for a period occupy, at any time in that period, a part of the space occupied by another particular of the kind at the time. This relation between particulars will hold whenever one particular is a physical part of another for a part or the whole of the history of either; a relation which is doubtless more commonly found between particulars of different kinds than between particulars of the same kind. Of any two particulars of the same kind it remains true that at any time at least part of one must be somewhere where no part of the other is at that time; and, hence, that no two such particulars can occupy just the same space-time tract.[6]

Particulars, then, are ultimately differentiated by spatio–temporal difference. What ultimately differentiates general concepts such as particulars exemplify? One may be tempted here by a metaphor which mimics the answer just given to the corresponding question about particulars. Thus one may say: every general concept occupies a position in *logical* space (or in *a* logical space), a position which it can wholly share with no other. This is not to say that one general concept cannot be wholly contained *within* the logical space occupied by another or wholly contain another within its logical space. And indeed both these relations can hold. The metaphor has some merit. Mimicking a symmetry, it proclaims an asymmetry. Attempting a parallel, it reveals a divergence. For a logical space is not a space.

A general concept, as earlier remarked, is capable in principle of being exemplified by any number of different particular instances. So concepts are principles of collection. But they are also principles of distinction. Concepts come in ranges; and what we want to retain from

---

[6] One might here be tempted to drop the qualification relating to kinds. But this would be a mistake. A man, a person, is not identical with his body; and though, normally, a man's body lasts longer than the man does, hence does not occupy exactly the same space–time tract as the man, yet if a man ceased to exist because he was blown to smithereens, then his body would simultaneously cease to exist and it might reasonably be held that he and his body would have occupied exactly the same space–time tract.

our metaphor is the notion of mutual logical exclusiveness within a range. To illustrate the notion of a range: the concepts of lion, tiger, panther, belong to one range, the feline animal-species range; the concept of yellow, red, blue, to another, that of colour or hue; of lying, standing, sitting, say, to another (physical attitude); of being completely surrounded by, being to the right of, being to the left of, being above, below, on a level with, to another (possible) range; of being square circular, triangular, to another. In the terms of our metaphor we think of the range as a (logical) space divided between the concepts which make up the range. What ultimately differentiates one concept from another in the range is just the space that it occupies in the range. But of course a logical space is not a space. What is meant is that the concepts of a range are principles of distinction among the particulars that come within the range, and are in logical competition with other members of the range throughout their field of application to particulars. If any particular (fairly and squarely) exemplifies one member of the concept-range, then there are other members of the range (or at least one other member) which that particular is thereby logically excluded from exemplifying. Of course there are borderline cases and (sometimes) hybrids. But our recognition of them *as such* only serves to emphasize the function of concepts as principles of distinction within the range.

And here we come to a quite fundamental respect of asymmetry between spatio–temporal particulars and the general concepts they exemplify. Consider on the one hand a set of concepts belonging to a given range and, on the other, the entire field of particulars which come within that range. Then, for any concept of the range, we know there are other concepts which are in logical competition with it throughout the field, i.e. no particular which exemplifies it can at the same time exemplify its competitors. But we can form no symmetrically competitive range of particulars. Indeed we cannot find a single particular such that there is any other single particular which competes with it for concepts throughout the concept-ranges they both come within. There are no two simultaneously existing particulars so related that from the fact that one exemplifies a concept, it follows, for every concept, that the other does not exemplify it (or does not exemplify it simultaneously).

We might express this, somewhat as I have done elsewhere,[7] by

[7] See 'The Asymmetry of Subjects and Predicates' in *Logico-Linguistic Papers*, London, Methuen, 1971, pp. 96–115.

saying that concepts of particulars come in incompatibility-groups in relation to particulars but particulars do not come in incompatibility-groups *vis-à-vis* concepts.

It might be said: this is insufficiently explained by saying that concepts are principles of distinction among particulars. For, after all, we could view particulars as principles of distinction among concepts. In relation to any given particular at any time, we could sort concepts into those it exemplified at that time and the rest. For an answer to this it is enough to revert to our question of the form: what ultimately differentiates one particular from another, one general concept from another? Concepts are ultimately differentiated just *as* the principles of distinction among particulars that they are. But particulars could not begin to serve as principles of distinction among concepts unless we had some other way of identifying and differentiating them. We identify them under concepts of kind of particular and ultimately differentiate them by their spatio-temporal relations, by their exclusive occupation of a tract of physical space–time. When we say, in metaphorical parallel with this, that concepts are ultimately differentiated by the exclusive occupancy of a position in a logical space, it is precisely the point that they come in incompatibility groups that is thereby made.

Now we turn to the other part of the metaphorical parallel. One particular may be a physical part of another, as an arm of a body, or include another as a part, as the arm includes the forearm. One concept, we say, may be wholly included in a part of the region of logical space occupied by another or contain another within a part of its logical space. Thus the region of logical space occupied by the concept *red* includes as a part that occupied by *scarlet* and is included in that occupied by *coloured* (here opposed, say, to *black-and-white* or to *colourless*). Once again the spatial terminology translates into the terminology of logical, though not formally logical, relation. Whatever particular is in question, its exemplifying the concept *red* would be a necessary condition of its exemplifying the concept *scarlet*, though not conversely; and its exemplifying the concept *red* would be a sufficient condition of exemplifying the concept *coloured*, though not conversely. We can find no particulars so related that, whatever concept was in question, the fact that one of those particulars exemplified that concept would be either a necessary or a sufficient condition of the other's doing so too (though not conversely). We can indeed find some particulars where this relation holds for *some* concepts; notably in the case of particulars themselves related by the part-whole relation. If my arm is uniformly tanned, then my forearm must be uniformly tanned. But if my arm is bent in the middle, it does not follow that my forearm is bent in the middle.

We might express this, somewhat as I have done elsewhere,[8] by saying that some concepts stand to others in one-way involvement relations *vis-à-vis* all particulars that come within their range, whereas no particulars stand in one-way involvement relations *vis-à-vis* all concepts whose ranges they come within.

Let me recall why this discussion of the general relative natures of spatio–temporal particulars and the general concepts they exemplify was undertaken. We were to inquire into the general relative natures of the terms combined in the 'basic combination' of predication. We supposed that the duality of subject and predicate must reflect some fundamental features of our thought about the world. We have seen that our thought about the world involves, at a level which, if not the most primitive of all, is yet primitive enough, the duality of spatio–temporal particular and general concept. To bring these two dualities together may illuminate both. More especially, the asymmetries just discussed, of particular and concept, may explain the formal differences, earlier set out, of subject and predicate. Discussion of those asymmetries already implicitly involved reference to certain types of judgment; for to talk of incompatibility or involvement of concepts is already to talk implicitly of relations between judgments of a certain sort. Any judgment to the effect that a certain spatio–temporal particular (or pair or trio, etc., of such particulars) exemplifies a certain general concept, or—equivalently—to the effect that a certain general concept has application in the case of a certain spatio-temporal particular (or pair or trio, etc., of such particulars) would be a judgment of this sort. So the hypothesis suggests itself that the basic subject–predicate sentences are sentences apt for the voicing of such judgments. Evidently the hypothesis must be made more specific than this if it is to fulfil an explanatory purpose: roles must be allotted to sentence-parts as well as to the sentence over-all. This will shortly be done, in an unsurprising way. But we need some further preliminaries first.

3. Propositional combination: a tripartition of function

We have two equivalent descriptions, or general forms of description, of the content of a fundamental type of judgement. How might linguistic expression be given to such judgements? Here is a very general descrip-

[8] ibid.

tion of a way it might be done in the case of a judgment relating to a single particular:[9] combine two expressions, one specifying the particular in question and one specifying the concept in question, *in such a way* that the result of the combination is true, or expresses a truth, if the particular exemplifies the concept—or, if the concept applies to the particular—and is false, or expresses a falsehood, if it does not.

This description is to be so understood that the following three things are required to be true of any sentence that falls under it: (1) there is contained in the sentence an expression specifying the particular in question; (2) there is contained in the sentence an expression specifying the general concept in question; (3) there is something contained in the sentence as a whole, or some feature of the mode of combination of the two aforementioned expressions, which shows that we have a truth-or-falsity-yielding combination of the sort just described, i.e. a combination which yields truth if the particular exemplifies the concept —or, if the concept applies to the particular—and falsity if not. A truth-or-falsity-yielding combination we call a propositional combination.

By one who understood the word 'concept' in a sense akin to that in which Frege used it, this tripartition of functions to be performed in a sentence of the kind concerned might be questioned on the ground that function of concept-specification really included what has just been represented as the distinguishable function of indicating propositional combination. But we do not here understand the word 'concept', or the function of concept-specification, in any such sense. Rather we understand them in such a way that, e.g., the concept *green* can equally be said to be specified in each of the three following English sentences: 'The door is green', 'The green door is locked', 'Green is a soothing colour'; and also in the clause itself which precedes the quoted sentences.

The three requirements listed above are, then, distinct requirements. Yet their separate listing might conceivably lead to a confusion which it is important to avoid. For every sentence which answers to the three requirements, it is clearly possible to frame an equivalent sentence, more elaborately composed, with the following features:

(1) it contains a *pair* of expressions, one specifying the particular in question and one specifying the general concept in question;

[9] For simplicity's sake I thus confine description at this point; but the description could readily be adapted to cases of judgment relating to pairs, trios, etc., of particulars.

21

(2) it contains an expression specifying a certain relational concept, viz. the concept of *exemplification* (or that of *application*);

(3) there is something contained in the sentence as a whole, or something about the mode of combinations of the aforementioned expressions, which shows that we have a propositional combination of the first *pair* of expressions with the expression specifying the concept of exemplification (or of application).

Now to say that a sentence satisfies the three requirements as initially listed is not to say that it is a sentence of the kind just described. In particular, it is not to say that it contains an expression specifying the concept of exemplification (or that of application). And of course this is really obvious enough; for if propositional combination could never be indicated without further concept-specification, we should be faced with an infinite regress.

So, to summarize. In any ground-level linguistic expression of a judgment of our fundamental type we distinguish three functions: that of specifying the particular(s) concerned; that of specifying the general concept concerned (i.e. the general concept which the particular(s) is (are) judged to exemplify); and that of presenting particular(s) and general concept as assigned to each other in such a way that you have a propositional combination, true if the particular (or pair, trio, etc.) exemplifies the concept, false if not.[10] The warning just given is a warning against supposing that in mentioning this last function, one is mentioning a further concept (e.g. that of exemplification) to be specified in the linguistic expression of the judgment.

4. Formal differences explained for the basic case

We have the hypothesis that the basic class of subject–predicate sentences is a class of sentences in which particular-specifying expressions and general-concept-specifying expressions are propositionally combined, i.e. combined in such a way as to yield truth if the particular (or couple, etc.) exemplifies the concept, falsity otherwise; and we have a consequential description of three functions to be allotted to parts or features of such a sentence. If our hypothesis is to be used to explain the formal differences of subject-terms and predicate-terms, we must

---

[10] This statement of truth-or-falsity conditions is clearly inadequate in so far as no mention is made of ordering of pairs, etc.; but I wish to avoid burdening the discussion with complications which have no relevance to this stage of it. The matter is discussed in Part Two, Chapter 3, Section 3.

make it more specific. It must include an at least partial allotment of functions to terms.

We enlarge our hypothesis, then, to include the provision that the sentence-part(s) specifying the particular(s) in question is (are) the subject-term(s), and that the sentence-part which specifies the concept in question is the predicate-term. The philosophical interest does not lie in this enlargement itself, which is quite generally assumed without question or consideration. It lies in the hope that, given the hypothesis, then the points we have before us about concepts, particulars and their mutual assignment in language will be seen to constitute the rationale, the underlying ground, of the formal features of predication.

I. RESTRICTION OF PREDICATES

Obviously, on our hypothesis, the first formal distinction of subject-terms and predictate-terms presents no problem of explanation at all, as far as the basic class of subject–predicate propositions is concerned. For, as earlier remarked, general concepts such as particulars may exemplify divide, in different ways, into different sorts: thinking of them as principles of collection of particulars, we may divide them into those which collect single particulars, those which collect pairs of particulars, those which collect trios, etc. But there is no particular which is not collected both under singleton-collecting principles and under pair-collecting and trio-collecting principles as well. This answers exactly, on our hypothesis, to the requirement that in a complete sentence of the class in question there should be just one predicate-term and that such a term should always require complementing with a fixed number of subject-terms; whereas subject-terms are not restricted to occurrence in sentences with a fixed number of terms.

2. NEGATIVE AND COMPOUND PREDICATES

The second formal distinction between subject- and predicate terms consisted in the fact that we could enrich our logic, at least as far as monadic predicates are concerned, with negative and compound predicate-terms; but could do no such thing for subject-terms. On our hypothesis this distinction can be both established and explained, for the basic class of subject–predicate propositions, by invoking the asymmetry between concept and particular in respect of the possession of incompatibility and involvement ranges. The argument follows.

Since concepts typically stand in these relations (of incompatibility and involvement) with other concepts, we can coherently enrich our stock of concepts by framing or defining new ones in terms of these relations. So there is no theoretical reason why we should not define, for any concept, its complementary concept: one which covers the whole of the logical space left unoccupied by the concept of which it is the complement; or, in other words, the concept which is not only incompatible with the original concept, but is also such that there is no logical room for a third concept incompatible with both. And there is every practical reason why, if we do introduce such a concept, we should represent it linguistically in a way which displays its logical character, i.e. by affixing a negation sign to the expression specifying the original concept. The resulting complex expression, when propositionally combined with a particular-specifying expression, is, on our hypothesis, a predicate. And the propositional combination of this predicate with a given subject is equivalent to the negation of the propositional combination of the predicate specifying the original concept with the given subject. So, in introducing such a term, we have introduced a negative predicate. But there can be no parallel procedure for introducing negative subjects into subject–predicate propositions of our basic class. For particulars do not stand to other particulars in such relations as concepts stand in to other concepts.[11]

Before turning to predicate-composition, it may be well to consider two queries about predicate-negation. First, how realistic is the above as a picture of any procedure we actually follow? As a picture of a procedure, it is not very realistic. For though with the help of the prefix 'non-', we do form some negative terms which may figure in predicate-place, we do not form many such terms in this way. But what is in question is not so much a procedure as an option: the option of construing many an ordinary subject–predicate sentence containing the word 'not' as involving predicate-negation instead of construing it as involving propositional negation.[12] To construe a term in such a sentence as a negative predicate is to construe it as having just the same logical character as would belong to a term, containing a negation sign, which was specifically introduced to express the complement of a given concept. The ground of the fact that the option is open to us is the same as the ground of the fact that the procedure is open to us.

[11] The argument for negative predicates, as opposed to negative subjects, is set out at greater length and in a somewhat different way in my article 'The Asymmetry of Subjects and Predicates' in *Logico-Linguistic Papers*, pp. 96–115.

[12] Construal here may be construed, if preferred, as paraphrase—into the logical language. The option is that of representing the form of the sentence by '$\bar{F}a$' instead of by '$-(\bar{F}a)$.'

The second query concerns the notion of a range, and also that of the complementary of a given concept. The notion of ranges of concepts within which incompatibility and/or involvement relations hold was not defined, but simply illustrated. But the question arises whether the complement of a given concept is to be thought of as covering the whole of conceptual space except for the area occupied by the given concept or simply the remainder of the conceptual space *inside some limited range* within which the given concept falls. If the latter, then we must think that not every attempt at propositional combination of subject-term and predicate-term results in a well-formed sentence, since, without appropriate limits on well-formedness, we should lose the equivalence of propositional negation and predicate-negation for our subject–predicate sentences, and thus destroy the whole notion of negative predicates as we have understood them. Now it might seem that we must come to a decision on this matter; and that if the decision were to go in favour of the latter or limiting alternative, then we should need a theory of ranges and of range-relations, a theory, in fact, of categories. But this is not so. For we can explain complementarity of concept in a way compatible with any decision we might come to. Generally, if F is a concept and a a particular and the propositional combination of an expression specifying a and an expression specifying F is well-formed, then the complementary concept of F covers all the logical space in any part of which there is room for any concept such that the propositional combination of an expression specifying a and an expression specifying that concept would be well-formed and would be incompatible with the propositional combination of an expression specifying a and an expression specifying F. This explanation allows scope for difference of opinion on the limits of well-formedness while preserving, for every possible decision, the equivalence we need.[13]

Now to turn to predicate-composition. I introduce, first, a little simple symbolism. I represent the three functions of particular-specification, concept-specification and propositional combination (or mutual assignment of particular and concept) by the form

ass $(i\ c)$

where 'i' represents particular-specification, 'c' concept-specification and 'ass (   )' propositional combination. I represent the propositional

[13] My own decision would be to impose no limits such as are here envisaged. See Part Two, pp. 81–2.

negation of such a combination by writing a negation-sign over the 'ass' of mutual assignment, thus;

$$\overline{\mathrm{ass}}\,(i\,c).$$

It is to be remembered that 'ass (   )' merely represents the function of propositional combination; it is not to be thought that 'ass' itself represents a concept-specifying expression, e.g. an expression specifying the concept of assignment or that of exemplification or that of application. (Here I repeat the warning given in section 3 above.)

Using this symbolism, we can present the case for negative predicates as follows. The complementary concept c_2 of a given concept c_1 is defined by means of the following necessary equivalence:

$$\overline{\mathrm{ass}}\,(i\,c_1) \leftrightarrow \mathrm{ass}\,(i\,c_2).$$

But we can dispense with any such definitions by adopting a standard formal means of representing the relationships which would be invoked in such definitions. So we represent the complement of any given concept by associating the negation sign directly with the expression specifying the given concept; and thus have the quite general form of equivalence:

$$\overline{\mathrm{ass}}\,(i\,c_1) \leftrightarrow \mathrm{ass}\,(i\,\bar{c_1}).$$

The procedure for predicate-composition is parallel. Because concepts typically stand in one-way involvement relations with other concepts, we can coherently define concepts related in more complex ways to other concepts. Given two concepts, c_1 and c_2, which are not incompatible with each other and which are such that the propositional combination of either with an expression specifying some particular is well-formed, we can define the concept c_3 which is the concept which is involved by c_1 and c_2 jointly and which involves each of c_1 and c_2 separately. That is to say, c_3 is defined by the following relations:

$$(\mathrm{ass}\,(i\,c_1)\,\&\,\mathrm{ass}\,(i\,c_2)) \rightarrow \mathrm{ass}\,(i\,c_3)$$
$$\mathrm{ass}\,(i\,c_3) \rightarrow \mathrm{ass}\,(i\,c_1)$$
$$\mathrm{ass}\,(i\,c_3) \rightarrow \mathrm{ass}\,(i\,c_2)$$

which, taken together, amount to:

$$(\mathrm{ass}\,(i\,c_1)\,\&\,\mathrm{ass}\,(i\,c_2)) \leftrightarrow \mathrm{ass}\,(i\,c_3).$$

c_3 is the conjunctive concept of c_1 and c_2. But we can dispense with any such definitions by utilizing a standard formal means of representing the relationships which would be invoked in such definitions. The obvious device is to use the conjunction sign of propositional logic to combine into a single compound concept-specifying expression the expressions which severally specify the original concepts. To do this is, on our hypothesis, to introduce a form of compound (conjunctive) predicate. It yields the perfectly general equivalence:

$$(\text{ass } (i\, c_1) \,\&\, \text{ass } (i\, c_2)) \leftrightarrow \text{ass } (i\, (c_1 \,\&\, c_2)).$$

Similarly, instead of defining, for given concepts, c_1 and c_2, their disjunctive concept, c_3, by means of the following relations:

$$\text{ass } (i\, c_1) \rightarrow \text{ass } (i\, c_3)$$
$$\text{ass } (i\, c_2) \rightarrow \text{ass } (i\, c_3)$$
$$(\text{ass } (i\, c_3) \,\&\, \overline{\text{ass } (i\, c_1)}) \rightarrow \text{ass } (i\, c_2)$$
$$(\text{ass } (i\, c_3) \,\&\, \overline{\text{ass } (i\, c_2)}) \rightarrow \text{ass } (i\, c_1)$$

which, taken together, amount to

$$(\text{ass } (i\, c_1) \lor \text{ass } (i\, c_2)) \leftrightarrow \text{ass } (i\, c_3),$$

we introduce a form of compound (disjunctive) concept-specifying expression, and have the perfectly general formal equivalence:

$$(\text{ass } (i\, c_1) \lor \text{ass } (i\, c_2)) \leftrightarrow \text{ass } (i\, (c_1 \lor c_2)).$$

Thereby, on our hypothesis, we introduce disjunctive predicates.

The essential underlying points of the foregoing argument are that, as far as the terms of basic subject–predicate propositions are concerned, a certain procedure makes sense in application to predicate-terms while there is no symmetrical procedure which makes sense in application to subject-terms; and that this is so because, on our hypothesis, predicate-terms specify concepts while subject-terms specify particulars, and concepts typically stand in incompatibility and involvement relations with other concepts *vis-à-vis* particulars in general, while no particular stands in such relations with any other particular *vis-à-vis* concepts in general. And the reason for this in turn is held to lie in the general nature of particulars and concepts, in the points already set out regarding the identity and differentiation of particulars on the one hand and the identity and differentiation of concepts on the other.

Yet these reasonings might not completely satisfy. It might be acknowledged that no particulars of kinds ordinarily recognized were the complementaries of ordinarily recognized particulars or the disjunctive or conjunctive particulars of such particulars; and yet suggested that it might be possible, without breaking altogether with the idea of a particular as something ultimately identified in spatio–temporal terms, to recognize new types of particular, introduced in relation to particulars of types ordinarily recognized but having just these unusual relations to them. What would be wrong, it might be asked, with simply *defining*, for a given particular, i_1, its complementary particular, i_2, as that for which the following equivalence holds for all concept-specifications:

$$\overline{\text{ass}}\,(i_1\,c) \leftrightarrow \text{ass}\,(i_2\,c)\ ?$$

Or again, why should we not, for a given pair of particulars, i_1 and i_2, define the conjunctive particular of the pair, i_3, as that for which the following equivalence similarly holds:

$$(\text{ass}\,(i_1\,c)\ \&\ \text{ass}\,(i_2\,c)) \leftrightarrow \text{ass}\,(i_3\,c)$$

and then the disjunctive particular of the pair, i_4, as that for which the following holds:

$$(\text{ass}\,(i_1\,c)\ \vee\ \text{ass}\,(i_2\,c)) \leftrightarrow \text{ass}\,(i_4\,c)\ ?$$

If these procedures were admissible, then on our hypothesis associating subject and predicate with particular-specifier and concept-specifier, negative and compound subject-terms would be perfectly in order.

It is obvious, however, that these procedures are not admissible; for they lead directly to absurd results. The complementary particular of any given particular, for example, will have to exemplify all the concepts which the given particular does not exemplify. But since some of these will be mutually incompatible, this is impossible. So no particular has a complementary. Again, it is clear that there can be no disjunctive or conjunctive particular of any pair of particulars of which one exemplifies a concept which the other does not exemplify. For the disjunctive particular of any such pair would have to exemplify both that concept and its complement, which is impossible. And the conjunctive particular would have to exemplify neither that concept nor its complement, which is also impossible.

This might be thought sufficient to cause us to lose interest in conjunctive or disjunctive particulars. But the matter can be pursued a little further. At present we have it that at most there could be conjunctive or disjunctive particulars only of pairs of particulars which were such that each member of the pair exemplified all concepts which the other exemplified, i.e. possessed all *general* properties, however complex, which the other possessed. But the existence of such pairs would at best be possible only in a strictly symmetrical or in an infinitely cyclical universe. But then what in such a universe would be the difference between the conjunctive particular of such a pair and the disjunctive particular of that pair? We could scarcely say they were differentiated positionally, as the members of the pair are. For what would this difference be? Nor can we escape trouble by saying that the conjunctive would be identical with the disjunctive particular. The positional question still cannot be shelved. For the disjunctive and conjunctive particular(s) must *have* a position in order to satisfy the requirements of concept-exemplification imposed by their (or its) logical character. Indeed they (or it) must have just the same *kind* of position (i.e. possess just the same general kind of positional relations) as the individual particulars of which they are supposed to be the disjunctive and/or conjunctive particulars. The truth is that even in this fanciful case, which is the only case in which they escape being obviously self-contradictory, our disjunctive and conjunctive particulars face, in a very grave form, the characteristic problem of our time: an identity-problem. Only *their* identity-problem is insoluble. They are in fact non-entities.

3. NOUN-PHRASE AND VERB-PHRASE

The third formal difference between subject and predicate appeared finally, when we sought a precise expression for it, as no more than the formal-grammatical (and perhaps linguistically parochial) point that in a logically subject–predicate sentence in English the subject was a noun or noun-phrase whereas the predicate was a verb or verb-phrase. Thus simple subject–predicate sentences such as 'Socrates swims' and 'Socrates is brave' are to be divided up into 'Socrates' as subject in each case and 'swims' or 'is brave' as predicate.

Now in our ground-level subject–predicate sentences in which particular(s)-specifiers and concept-specifiers are propositionally combined, we have distinguished three functions of which only two, on our working hypothesis, have so far been allotted. The three functions are those of: (1) particular-specification; (2) concept-specification; and (3) indicating propositional combination (or predicative linkage or mutual assignment). The hypothetical allotment of the first two functions creates no disharmony with the formal-grammatical principle of division just mentioned; for the noun 'Socrates' specifies the assigned particular man and hence is functionally subject, while the verb-phrases 'swims' and 'is brave', whatever else they may do, respectively specify the assigned concepts of swimming and bravery and hence are functionally predicates.

But now what of the third function, that of indicating propositional combination? If our ground-level subject–predicate sentences are to be divided exhaustively into subject- and predicate-terms, as the formal–grammatical division requires, then this third function must be allotted to one of these two parts or be held to be performed simply by the fact, or the manner, of their being brought together. To which, then, of these two parts, if to either, should we attribute the performance of this function? There can scarcely be any doubt about the answer. We should ascribe this function to what, on other functional grounds, we have already identified as the predicate, 'swims' or 'is brave'; and we should do so because these expressions have the form of the verb or verb-phrase. Of course the predicate-expression cannot perform the combining function without an attendant or juxtaposed expression to combine with. The grappling machinery needs something to grapple. But there seems no doubt that we locate that machinery on the side of the verb-phrase rather than that of the noun-phrase.

Given this association of the form of the verb with the function of indicating propositional combination, we can define our explanatory task for the third formal distinction between subject and predicate. The task is that of explaining why, when particular-specifying expression and concept-specifying expression are propositionally combined, the function of indicating propositional combination should be associated with that of concept-specifying rather than with that of particular-specifying. It is to be noted that this association is not absolutely compelling. The intelligibility of the symbolism already used, viz., 'ass $(i\ c)$', in which the three functions in question are separately represented, would be sufficient indication of that, if any such indication were needed. But given that the association exists, we have the task of explaining it; and this is the task set us by the third formal distinction.

The explanation proceeds by way of the notion of negation. Concepts and particulars being what they are, we know that, given our working hypothesis, we can have negative predicates but not negative subjects. So when it is a question of framing a formal contradictory for a proposition of our fundamental kind, we have two ways open to us: that of negating the sentence as a whole which expresses the proposition or that of negating the concept-specifying expression which is its predicate. Now in using the above-mentioned symbolism, which separates the three functions concerned, we indicated negation of the whole sentence by taking a negation sign with the symbolism of propositional combination, 'ass', writing the form '$\overline{ass}\,(i\,c)$'. Nothing, certainly, is more natural than this. The symbolism of propositional combination serves to show that we have a certain sort of combination of the particular-specifying expression and the concept-specifying expression, viz., a combination which yields truth under one set of conditions and falsity under another. The effect of negating the proposition is simply to reverse (or exchange) the connections between these truth-values and these conditions. Nothing is more natural than to indicate this effect by, as it were, changing the sign of the propositional indicator, of whatever indicates that we have a truth-or-falsity-yielding combination. Thus, to modify a suggestion of Ramsey's, we might write 'ass' upside down or backwards; or, as here, introduce an extra sign in association with it. So negation and the symbolism of propositional combination have a natural affinity for each other. But we have lately been engaged in demonstrating, among other things, the affinity of concept-specification and negation for each other. So here we have, as regards our basic class of subject–predicate sentences, a mediated or resultant affinity between the function of indicating propositional combination and the concept-specifying function; hence an explanation, or partial explanation, of why predicates have the form of the verb. We might put it like this: the 'ass' function and negation are at home together; if negation can be absorbed into the predicate, conceived as that part of the combination which has the concept-specifying role, then the 'ass' function can be absorbed into it too.

I do not say that this way through negation is the only way to explain the affinity for each other of the concept-specifying function and that of indicating propositional combination; and hence to explain why the predicate has the form of the verb. Other considerations can be brought to bear.[14] Yet I think it is a way which takes us very near to the heart of the matter; and it illumines that dim suggestiveness, already noted, to be found in the first, corrigible formulation, turning on 'true of' and 'false of', of the third formal distinction.

[14] See, for example, the theory of completeness and incompleteness developed in *Individuals*, London, Methuen, 1959.

4. ACCESSIBILITY OF POSITIONS TO QUANTIFIERS

We now have to explain an alleged further formal difference between subject-terms and predicate-terms. We have to explain the doctrine that the position occupied by subject-terms in subject-predicate sentences is accessible to quantifiers, or to variables of quantification, while the position occupied by predicate-terms is not. It is not here a question of explaining why this is so, for it is not so; but of explaining why it is thought to be so. And the key point in the explanation is the point that predicates, in our fundamental class of sentences, have the double function just remarked on: the function of specifying the assigned concept *and* the function of indicating propositional assignment.

Let us consider again our two simple sentences: (a) 'Socrates swims'; (b) 'Socrates is brave'. They yield, by generalization, the sentences 'Someone swims' and 'Someone is brave' or 'There is someone who swims' and 'There is someone who is brave'; and here the particular-specifying expression 'Socrates' gives up its place to the unspecific 'Someone' or 'There is someone who'. According to the doctrine in question, our sentences (a) and (b) cannot similarly yield by generalization the sentences 'Socrates does something' (or 'There is something Socrates does') and 'Socrates is something' (or 'There is something Socrates is'). For to allow that they did so would be to allow quantification into predicate-place. We are offered, however, another possibility. If we are prepared to abandon the ground-level form of the sentences (a) and (b), to specify our concepts by nouns instead of by verb-phrases and to introduce some suitable two-place predicate, *then* we can proceed to generalize, to eliminate specificity in favour of non-specificity, in a way perfectly consistent with the doctrine. Sentences on the lines of

$$\text{(A) Socrates} \begin{cases} \text{performs} \\ \text{does} \\ \text{exemplifies} \end{cases} \text{swimming}$$

or of

$$\text{(B) Socrates} \begin{cases} \text{possesses} \\ \text{has} \\ \text{exemplifies} \end{cases} \text{bravery}$$

have attribute-naming nouns, 'swimming' or 'bravery', in referential or subject-position, coupled by a *new two-place predicate* with the name

'Socrates', also in subject-position; and the position of these names can safely be yielded to the non-specific 'something' or 'there is something which'. For when the names go, they leave a predicate behind; and (the phrase is Quine's) *predicates are wanted in all sentences*.[15]

The phrase casts a flood of light on the doctrine; but what it reveals is a confusion. What is wanted in all sentences (of a propositional kind) is an indication of propositionality, the verb-form or whatever does its duty. It is no more necessary that sentences should contain predicates in the full sense which entails concept-specification than it is that they should contain subjects in the full sense which entails individual-specification. So 'Socrates does something' (or 'Socrates is something') is just as good, *and just as direct*, a generalization from 'Socrates swims' (or 'Socrates is brave') as 'Someone swims' (or 'Someone is brave') is. The phrase 'does something' ('is something') replaces specificity with non-specificity just as the prase 'someone' does. It also exhibits the form of the verb, necessary for sentencehood (propositionality). It is the failure to see, or the refusal to acknowledge, that ordinary predicate-expressions *combine* the function of concept-specification with that of propositional indication that is, after all, responsible for the restriction which the doctrine imposes on quantification.

To establish the point, it should be enough to note a certain absurd consequence of the doctrine. If the doctrine is to be more than an arbitrary *fiat*, the formal difference between the pair of sentences (a) and (b) and some pair from sentences (A) and (B) must be a mark of some more substantial difference between them, which accounts for the fact that the latter pair permit of generalization in a way for which there is no parallel in the case of the former pair. The formal difference cannot be simply a matter of stylistic variation. It must have a deeper significance. And indeed it is made clear enough what this deeper significance is supposed to be. The idea is that (A) or (B) *commit* us, as regards swimming and bravery, in a way in which we are not at all committed by (a) 'Socrates swims' or by (b) 'Socrates is brave'.

But this is absurd. The theory of 'commitment' by noun, but not by adjective or verb, is as absolutely implausible as any philosophical view could be. We are just as much 'committed' by (a) and (b) as we are by (A) and (B). Let us say, if we will, that one who says 'Socrates exemplifies (possesses) bravery' thereby 'brings in' the attribute or concept, *bravery*, or shows himself as acknowledging this attribute or concept. But then let us add that one who says 'Socrates is brave' brings in the

15 *The Philosophy of Logic*, p. 28.

attribute or concept, *bravery*, just as much as one who says 'Socrates possesses bravery'.

Why should the absurd view be held? For answer, we turn to the same point as before. The fact that the predicate always incorporates the propositional symbolism of the verb makes it easier to overlook or become blind to the fact that it also specifies a concept or attribute quite as fully and completely as any noun could. It is the former fact that makes it possible to slide away from the specificatory function of the predicate by way of such a slogan as: predicates are just *true or false of* what subject-terms stand for. But this soothing, pacifying and deceptive phrase, in so far as it makes any clear point at all, simply makes the point that predicate-phrases incorporate the propositional symbolism, the symbolism of the verb. It is the same fact, and the same ensuing blindness, which accounts for that other revealing slogan, 'Predicates are wanted in all sentences', and hence for the denial that predicate-place can be yielded up, as subject-place can be yielded up, to quantification.

It will be seen that the sequence of explanations, or partial explanations, (2), (3) and (4), exhibits a certain order of dependence. The feature explained at an earlier stage is itself used in the explanation which follows. The feature explained at (2) was that predicates admitted of negation and composition and subjects did not. On our quite unoriginal hypothesis regarding a certain class of subject–predicate propositions, this feature was explained, for that class, by the contrast between particulars and their concepts in respect of the possession of incompatibility and involvement ranges *vis-à-vis* each other. The fact that predicates as concept-specifiers admitted of negation and subjects as particular-specifiers did not, once explained, was then itself brought into service to help explain why the concept-specifying part of the proposition should also, at least in languages known to us, be the part that carries the propositional indication; i.e. to explain why the predicate has the form of the verb. Then, finally, the fact that the predicate has this double function—of concept-specification and propositional indication—was used to cast at least some light on the question why it should be thought that predicate-place is not, as such, accessible to generalization.

On a certain hypothesis, then, regarding a certain class of subject–predicate propositions, we have now been able to explain, as far as that class of propositions is concerned, the formal differences between subjects and predicates—or, in one case, the supposition of a difference—

which were listed at the outset. The class of subject–predicate propositions in question is the class of those propositions in which a particular-specifying term (or terms) is propositionally combined with a term specifying a general concept such as particulars (or couples or trios of particulars) may exemplify; and the hypothesis is that the subject-term(s) specifies (specify) the particular(s) in question, the predicate-term the concept in question. Obviously, the *general* explanatory task we set ourselves at the outset is not completed. For the explanation we have applies only to a restricted class of propositions, included in, but not co-extensive with, the class of subject–predicate propositions in general.

5. The generalization of the form

The general explanatory task is not yet completed. But if the explanation we have is accepted as adequate in principle for the class of subject-predicate propositions to which it applies, then we have not much further to go. For, as earlier considerations about judgment and experience suggest, there are good epistemological grounds for regarding our chosen class of subject–predicate propositions as the basic or fundamental class of such propositions. To accept that this class *is* fundamental and to accept the adequacy of our explanation for this class is, then, among other things, to accept that the basic or primary occupants of subject-position (subject-terms) are terms specifying particulars and the basic or primary occupants of predicate position (predicates) are terms specifying general concepts applicable to such particulars. Now an early and crucial explanatory step was to isolate a certain *contrast* between particulars and the general concepts they exemplify—a contrast we bring out by considering concepts and particulars in relation to each other and to the general possibility of propositions of our fundamental class. This was the contrast I expressed by saying that *concepts* come in incompatibility and involvement groups *vis-à-vis particulars* and *particulars* do not (and cannot) come in such groups *vis-à-vis concepts*. But this contrast is capable of generalization beyond this basic case of it. I have spoken of concepts of particulars as, among other things, principles of grouping of particulars. But these principles of grouping may themselves be grouped under higher principles to which they stand in the very same contrastive relation as particulars stand to the principles which group them. And we distinguish and group yet other things which are neither spatio–temporal particulars nor yet simple kind-principles, or quality-principles, of grouping particulars:

such as numbers or words or musical or literary compositions. And these things, too, stand to the concepts under which we group them in the same contrastive relation as spatio–temporal particulars stand to the concepts of kind or quality under which we group them. Thus we may assign *properties* to numbers and class musical or literary compositions according to their *kinds*. And the concepts of such properties and kinds come in incompatibility and involvement groups *vis-à-vis* numbers or compositions, while numbers or compositions do not come in such groups *vis-à-vis* their properties and kinds.

Moreover, just as the principles under which we group particulars may be principles of grouping, not single particulars, but pairs or trios of particulars, so the concepts exemplified by non-particulars may be principles of grouping, not single non-particulars, but pairs or trios of such.

These are powerful analogies. They form the sufficient ground of the possibility of singular propositions in which a term (or terms) specifying a non-particular (or non-particulars) and a term (expression) specifying a principle of grouping or collection of such non-particulars are combined in a way which is formally and grammatically quite analogous to the way in which a particular-specifying term and a concept-specifying term are combined in the basic class of subject–predicate propositions. And if we actually have such combinations, then of course we actually have subject–predicate propositions, though not of the basic class. And of course we do have such propositions. For example, '7 is prime'; '7 is greater than 5'; 'Green is soothing'; 'Green is a more soothing colour than orange'; 'This sonnet is Petrarchan'; 'This sonnet is more regular than that'; ' "Monotheistic" has five syllables'; ' "Monotheistic" has more letters than "unitarian" '. These are all of the form '*Fa*' or '*Fab*'. They have the same formal characteristics as the basic propositions of this form. The explanation of their possibility is, as I have said, that the logical contrast between particulars and the concepts particulars exemplify can be reproduced at a higher, more abstract, level; so the logical place which basically belongs to particular-specifiers can be occupied by non-particular-specifiers—when the latter are suitably accompanied. But we must not be so enchanted by the common logical contrast as to lose sight of the basic case of it, and of the fact that it is the basic case. Not, that is, if we want to understand the fundamental character of our thinking, and hence see our way through the philosophical perplexities that arise from not understanding it. The basic case is the model for the other cases. From this fact spring both the delusions of Platonism and the delusions of anti-Platonism. They are indeed, but two sides of the same delusion.

6. An objection answered

It seems a reasonable principle, in philosophy as elsewhere, that what is less clear should be explained in terms of what is clearer, and hence that explanation of some phenomenon of thought or its expression should not rest upon a notion as obscure as the phenomenon to be explained. The principle is not quite as simply compelling as at first it may seem. For philosophical explanation is not a steady, reductive movement in the direction of the intrinsically clear, but rather an exhibition of connections and relations between notions none of which is immediately transparent to philosophical understanding. The clarity is in the connections. Yet, so long as it is not naïvely interpreted, the principle must be allowed to have force, particularly where explanation makes a free use of terms of philosophical art. And it might be objected to much of the foregoing that far too free a use is made of the notions of a 'concept' and of 'specifying a concept'.

The objection, indeed, might take an extreme form which goes far beyond a complaint of lack of clarity. It might be held that the only reason, discernible in what has been said, for assuming that some terms specify concepts lies in the supposed explanatory fruitfulness of the assumption; and that, since we can score the same explanatory successes without it, we can simply drop the assumption; and that this will be an advantage, since the assumption is suspect anyway.

What we have to recognize, so the argument goes, is that the basic distinction of terms, in the sentences we are concerned with, is the distinction between those terms which, like '. . . loves . . .' and '. . . is bald', are essentially sentence-frames, requiring completion into sentences by the filling of the gaps they exhibit, and those terms such as 'Caesar' and 'Brutus', which are available for filling the gaps. To this contrast it might be objected that there is really no more reason for viewing 'loves' and 'is bald' as sentence-frames, viz. '. . . loves . . .' and '. . . is bald', than there is for viewing 'Caesar' and 'Brutus' in this way, say as 'Caesar . . .' or '. . . Brutus', since all these expressions equally fail in themselves to be complete sentences and all are equally capable of being completed into sentences. But the objection is superficial. For expressions of the former sort differ from expressions of the latter sort in that each of the former demands completion (into a complete unquantified sentence) in accordance with a fixed and unvarying pattern: its 'gaps' must be filled with a definite number, one or two or three, etc., of terms of the other sort. But this is not so with terms of the other sort. Any of them can figure in any pattern of sentence of the kind we are concerned with. They cannot be represented as bringing with them a definite number of gaps. So there is a good sense in which terms of the one sort can be said to be sentence-frames and in which terms of the other sort cannot.

This fundamental ground of distinction between predicate-terms and subject-terms—the argument continues—carries with it the explanation of another of the formal differences initially listed, viz. that predicate-terms have the form of the verb, or carry the indication of propositionality, while subject-terms do not. Naturally it is the sentence-frame, and not the fillings of that frame, which carries the marks of sentence-hood. And this brings with it another consequence. For it was remarked, in the course of the arguments earlier set out, that when we negate a proposition of the kind we are concerned with, it is natural to indicate negation by modifying whatever sentence-part carries the propositional indication. So, since predicates, being sentence-frames, carry this indication, they naturally admit of negation; which was another thing to be explained. It is then easy to demonstrate that the admission of negative predicates is compatible with the admission of conjunctive and disjunctive predicates and incompatible with the admission of conjunctive and disjunctive subjects.

The argument is still incomplete. The doctrine of accessibility of term-position to occupation by quantifiers has yet to be considered. We might imagine the argument completed as follows. The doctrine that predicate-position is inaccessible to quantifiers is sound! Precisely because predicates do not specify concepts or attributes or any such matters, they cannot yield up their place to the non-specifying signs of generalization. But subject-terms, the gap-fillers which do purport to name or specify, can yield up *their* place to the signs of non-specificity.

It will be apparent that the last, imagined stage of the argument—if there is to be any attempt to give an account of such legitimate and intelligible constructions as 'Socrates does something', 'Socrates is something', etc.—will be exposed to that charge of gross implausibility already levelled at the theory of commitment by noun, but not by adjective or verb. Let us waive the point, however, and consider the general character of the argument up to the last, imagined stage.

The first of the formal distinctions originally listed is incorporated into the initial characterization of subject- and predicate-terms and so is not to be explained at all, but is to be made the ground of whatever explanation is forthcoming of the other formal differences. The description adopted in the initial characterization is also very nearly such as to incorporate the third of the formal differences originally listed; for the first formal difference is exploited to justify the name 'sentence-frame' for predicate-expressions, and this name is then used to justify a very short step to propositional indication. Finally, as regards the asymmetry between subject-terms and predicate-terms in respect of negation and composition, though an explanatory connection with propositional indication is suggested in the case of negation, no independent explanation is offered for asymmetry in respect of composition, this feature being simply presented as a formal consequence of asymmetry in respect of negation.

If we again waive reference to the last imagined stage of the argument, we must surely be struck by two major characteristics of this account. The first is its purely formal-syntactic basis, the abjuring of any allusion to the semantic character of subject-terms or predicate-terms. The second is the thinness, the slightness, of its explanatory content. The two characteristics are connected. It is natural and reasonable to inquire what it is about the sort of *sense*, or the sort of *function* in sentences, or both, which the terms in question have, which accounts for the range of formal features the sentences present. And it is, of course, precisely this question which I have attempted to answer in the earlier sections of this chapter, making free use, for this purpose, of the notions of 'expressions specifying concepts' and 'expressions specifying particulars'.

We return, then, to the complaint that the notion of concept is obscure in a way in which that of spatio–temporal particular, perhaps, is not. The complaint may take a more specific form. Spatio–temporal particulars, it seems, are not the creatures of language; they have their own independent being in the world, owing nothing to words (except when they are utterances or inscriptions of words). But there is no hope of understanding what concepts are except by seeing them as the creatures of language. They owe their being, such as it is, to words. So how could one hope to explain, in any genuine and non-circular way, the functioning of expressions by reference to the nature of concepts? At best one could hope for a metaphorical representation of just what one seeks to explain.

The contrast is a good deal overdrawn. But let it stand. Let it be allowed that to talk of concepts is to talk of the *senses* of expressions. It is of just this that we need to talk in order to bring out that underlying asymmetry of basic subject- and predicate-terms which is the ground of so much else. Expressions designating particulars will never, while they perform this function, exhibit, *vis-à-vis* those general terms which complement them in a propositional combination, those relations *inter se* which general terms in such a combination will exhibit *vis-à-vis* them. And this is precisely a matter of the senses that such general terms have, senses of which our full or imperfect grasp is a full or imperfect grasp of principles of distinction or grouping among the items we encounter in space and time.

Scepticism may extend, has been extended, to the notion of sense or meaning as well. But scepticism, stretched so far, is over-stretched. For the application of logic itself requires that we are able to identify the same word in different occurrences; and this we cannot do without some notion of preservation of sense, which is something not guaranteed by recurrence of physical design. Even if we turn our backs on this thought, on the possibility of ambiguity, we can still see how very strange is the persistent illusion that to talk of words or expressions is to take one's stand on firm ground instead of trusting oneself to the bogs and swamps of universals, concepts and the rest. For even as sign-design, the same word must be identified in different occurrences, or different inscriptions identified as inscriptions of the same word. So grasp of the identity of a word involves grasp of a principle of grouping of inscriptions or utterances. How odd to think that one could escape acknowledgement of such principles by retreating to the ground of words! What a compounding of oddities indeed, given that another principle of grouping—the sense of the word—enters in fact into that very principle of grouping which we apply in identifying the word!

2
Proper Names - and Others

Subject–predicate propositions of the basic class are propositions in which particular-specifying expressions as subjects are propositionally combined with concept-specifying expressions as predicates. The description is somewhat abstract, and we must try to bring it closer to the facts of discourse. We must ask what linguistic means are available for framing, or expressing, such propositions and in what conditions the employment of such means is to count as framing such a proposition.

The question can be made more specific, for it primarily concerns subject-terms. We confront the linguistic facts, the total reality of actual discourse, with the sparse notation of logical grammar—not the very sparse notation favoured by Quine, which has no place for subject-terms, but the rather less sparse notation which keeps such a place— and ask: what are the cases, and what are the ways, in which, if we are to fit our discourse about particulars into this framework, we can do so with least forcing of the facts by making use of the option, available in the notation, of representing a fragment of discourse as a subject-term? I take some first steps in answering this question; I do not pursue it into all its ramifications.

1. What is the use of them?

The most obvious category of candidates for the role of subjects in our basic subject–predicate propositions is the category of proper names for particulars. Theories of names abound. We do well to approach discussion of the matter in a low key. And so my own discussion of this category of expressions will be, at least to begin with, of a very low-keyed and commonplace and non-theoretical order. It will also, for the matter is really one of great complexity, be partial and incomplete. But here, even more than elsewhere, I think, we have to bear in mind that *an understanding of linguistic function pre-eminently involves an understanding of the UTILITY of linguistic forms in communication between human beings variously circumstanced and variously equipped.*

I. CONDITIONS OF UTILITY FOR NAMES

One way of trying to get an initial grasp of the utility, and hence of the modes of functioning, of proper names for particulars would be to ask: what sorts of particulars characteristically have proper names? and why these sorts? and not others? If one asks the first of these questions, one is immediately struck by the fact that examples that first come to mind are above all names of *people* and of what might be called *places*. And it might seem potentially fruitful to inquire why this is so. We may get an answer to this as we go.

Again, we might ask: what sorts of general conditions are there under which we might expect a proper name for a spatio–temporal particular to have useful currency? Consider the following three conditions: (1) there is a circle or group of language-users among whom there is frequent need or occasion to make identifying reference to a certain particular; (2) there is an interest in the continuing identity of the particular from occasion to occasion of reference; (3) there is no short description or title of that particular which, because, say, of some fact about the relation of the particular to the members of that circle, is always available and natural within the circle as a constant means of identifying reference to that particular. These are surely conditions under which we might expect a proper name of that particular to have useful currency within that circle.

Is this an exhaustive statement of the conditions of the utility of proper names? It is not. But it indicates the right starting-point.

On the first condition I will, for the moment, say no more. The force of the second condition can be illustrated by considering the case of a group of bar billiards players who regularly use the same equipment. Its members may frequently have occasion to refer to what is in fact the same particular white ball, on many different occasions of reference. They constitute a group which, in relation to that ball, satisfies the first condition. There is no one constant and salient description of the ball; it has to be identified by position, whether demonstratively or descriptively, on each occasion of reference. So the third condition also is satisfied. But the fact of its being the same individual from occasion to occasion of reference is of no interest at all, indeed will pass, in general, unnoticed. So the second condition is not satisfied; and the ball is nameless.

We can best understand the third, negatively phrased condition by considering cases in which it is not fulfilled, i.e. cases in which there *is* a short description or title which, for some reason, is always available and natural within the circle as a constant means of referring to the particular in question. Consider ordinary class or general names like 'car', 'house', 'kitchen', 'baby'. Very often, one particular member of the relevant class is of paramount standing interest to the members of a given circle, say a family circle. For purposes of communication within that circle the general name itself, preceded by the definite article, will normally serve perfectly well for identification. Or again— a different sort of case—consider general names which indicate position in an organized community of some kind: Commanding Officer or Quartermaster in a regiment; chef, carpenter, or Master in an Oxford college; King or President in a state; and so on. For communication between members of the community such phrases as 'the C.O.', 'the carpenter', 'the Master', will again normally serve perfectly well for purposes of identification. In this type of case the particulars to be referred to are not in the same way things of different general kinds: they are all men. Now no doubt for each of them there are many things which characterize him uniquely, besides the fact that he occupies uniquely a certain position in the community in question; and no doubt there are many other men who occupy the same sort of position in other communities; but for the members of this community, at least when it is *as* members of this group that they are communicating with each other, this fact of his position will be salient or uppermost, will select itself as the identifying fact about him. This reliance on salient identifying facts about objects of the same basic kind is evidently rather different from the family circle case where the basic kind-name alone is enough.

Now let us consider a quite different kind of case, a case where the three conditions I mentioned *are* satisfied, but in a somewhat short-term

43

way. Suppose two people go to watch a team game, such as football or basketball. They have no real prior interest in the sport, they know nothing about its personalities and little about its procedures. They go for some extraneous reason—perhaps sociological: their object, say, is crowd observation. However, as they watch the game, they become interested in spite of themselves. They exchange comments. Among other things they find themselves wanting to refer repeatedly to an individual performer or two, bringing out the fact that it is the same one that they are referring to again and again. Having no standing interest in the sport, they do not know their names or the technical names of their positions. If they knew the latter, this would provide just the kind of salient fact we found in the case of the C.O. Of course from moment to moment one speaker could identify an individual player in terms of what he has just done or where he is on the field. But this, besides being cumbrous, would fail to register the point that it is the same player he keeps referring to. The two watchers, for the duration of the game and perhaps a little time afterwards, constitute now something like a name-needing circle in relation to the players concerned. And indeed they might solve their problem by importing, as it were, mock names on the strength, perhaps, of some fancied resemblance or idiosyncrasy of manners or dress. But the basis of the name, if it has any such basis, is quite unimportant. Once the name is established, it does not matter if they forget or lose sight of its basis altogether.

I call this 'something like a name-needing situation' because of the very restricted character of the circle and of its interest. We might call it a mini-name-needing situation. The watchers do not want to know the players' real names. They do not want to follow their careers. They will never see another game. Now it is quite likely, of course, that the authorities will have solved the watchers' referring problem for them by labelling the players with large numbers; though not with quite their problem in mind. This case is queer and instructive. Do not the large numbers on the backs supply us with just the kind of salient individuating facts about the players which I said dispensed with the need for names? Not quite. They are not facts of the same kind. The fact that a particular player whom they repeatedly want to refer to has a large No. 3 on his back is not in itself a fact of any interest about him; it is not that at all which engages our interest in him. (How different from the case of 'the baby', 'the car', 'the Master', 'the C.O.') It is just a convenience, given the independent need to make identifying references to him. We can even suppose it designed to meet this need. It is in a different class, then, from those descriptions I previously spoke of. So we might be inclined to think of it as like a proper name. Yet the number is not a proper name either. I shall come back later to a case somewhat like this.

Let me dwell for a moment more on the contrast between the game-situation and the case of the Commanding Officer. A phrase like 'the Commanding Officer' catches its man, so to speak, in a certain relation. As we have seen, it may be the most natural sort of expression to serve all the needs of identifying reference within a certain circle. He may get another appointment, of course, so that the expression, as used within the circle, no longer applies to him; but then he goes out of the life of the circle, its members no longer need to talk about him or, if they do, they can do so by qualifying the old expression and speak of 'the old C.O.'; and they can apply the old expression, perhaps at first also qualified—'the *new* C.O.'—to his successor. Compare this with the game situation, taking the game situation as a model, as it were, for the life situation. There, too, there were available identifying descriptions which caught their man in a particular position, in a particular relation, e.g. 'the man who's holding the ball now', 'the one who's just scored'. But these were no use to the speakers because, although it was only per-formance in the game that mattered to them, they wanted a designation which precisely did not depend on a particular momentary position or relation. So they imported mock names, or used the label thoughtfully provided by the authorities. Neglecting the label case, we may say that they named the player for the life span of the game.

Now to make the transition from the mock or mini-names of the model to real life or full-dress names. Evidently in the course of his life a man stands in many positions, in many relations, which might ade-quately serve different speakers-about-him, at different times, as the basis of economical enough identifying descriptions or titles. Evidently also, however, there may be overlapping groups of communicators-about-him with an interest in identifying reference to him, the members of which know him, or know of him, in perhaps many different sets of individuating relations, overlapping with each other; and have a con-tinuing interest in him, as one and the same person, an interest which extends over changes in such positions and relations. For them, there-fore, there can be no one overriding description which fulfils their *common* needs in the way in which 'the C.O.' does fulfil the needs of the circle I spoke of before. So it is convenient to have in circulation in such groups a tag, a designation, which does not depend for its referential or identifying force upon any particular such position or relation, which preserves the same referential force through its object's changes of position or relation and has the same referential force for communicators who know the object in different connections and for whom quite different descriptions would be uppermost. It is convenient, in fact, to have personal names; it is natural, given the character of our interest in, and needs to communicate identifyingly about, human beings, that we (i.e. any particular one of us) should use such names for some human beings we refer to, though not for others. And indeed for any human being there is likely to exist some group or groups of communicators-about-him, such that there is, for that group or groups, a need for a name for that human being.

I make no claim to have described exhaustively the nature of the need for personal names; only to have indicated something of its general character. Consider, for example, the case of a group of persons united exclusively by ties of personal knowledge or intimacy. Here the use of anything but a name in talk, within the group, about a member of it, would be very odd. We should think why this is so. It surely has to do with there being no one particular fact about any member, no particular relationship in which he stands, such that it is on account of that fact or relationship that he is a standing object of reference for members of this group. Compare this with the mixed case of a group of human beings who both stand in some set of public or official relations to each other, and are also bound by ties of personal knowledge and intimacy. In so far as their discourse about each other reflects this latter fact about them, they will tend to use names; there would be an unnaturalness, suggestive of irony, in referring to them by position. But this will not always be unnatural or inappropriate. Thus in the formal setting of a college meeting, for example (i.e. a meeting of those academics who constitute the governing body of a college) those same human beings who, talking to each other outside such a setting, refer to each other by name will quite naturally find themselves referring to each other as, say, the Dean, the Senior Tutor, the Law Tutor, etc.

2. CONDITIONS OF SUCCESSFUL USE OF NAMES

Now I want to remark on some conditions of a different kind—not the conditions of a name's general utility, but the conditions for the successful use of a name in identifying reference on a particular occasion. I have sometimes spoken of *identifying reference* to particular items as essentially drawing, or intended to draw, on resources of knowledge in the possession of the audience.[1] The need for a background of identifying knowledge seems nowhere more evident than in the case of names, though it is hard to state formally and generally what the character of this background must be. We can, it seems, at least say this: that the successful use of a name in communication requires that hearer and speaker should each understand the name, as used in that particular communication, as having a certain unique reference; and that the reference should be the same for each of them. In other words, each must know who *he* means, or understands, by the name, as then used; and each must mean or understand the same person. This we may treat as a defining requirement of 'successful use' as the phrase is here employed. What does it substantially involve?

One might be inclined to think that this condition involved at least the requirement that both participants in the conversation should have in common knowledge of at least one non-name-dependent identifying description of the person referred to. (By 'identifying description' I mean 'uniquely applicable description'; by 'non-name-dependent' I do not mean 'not including any name', I mean 'not including, or quoting, the very name in question'.) But there are several objections to regarding this requirement as necessarily involved by the defining condition.

First, in general, it seems in fact perfectly possible that, without there being any piece of non-name-dependent identifying knowledge common to both participants, yet there is only one person who is customarily referred to by the name in question *and* is known to, or known of by, both participants in the conversation *and* is such that each would presume the other to mean or understand that person by that name in that conversation.

Second, the idea of a bearer of a name being known to each participant in the conversation is too narrowly conceived if it is conceived solely in terms of knowledge of identifying descriptions. For one can perfectly well claim *command* of a name (i.e. claim to know who or what is meant by the use of a name) simply on the ground of ability to recognize its bearer when one perceptually encounters its bearer, even if one cannot produce any non-name-dependent identifying description of him or it; cannot, for example, say by what marks one distinguishes him, or report any particular occasion of encounter. A head of a college, a commander of troops or a M.F.H. might, in this sense only, *know* some of his undergraduates, men or hounds *by name*.

[1] See 'Singular Terms and Predication' and 'Identifying Reference and Truth-Values' in *Logico-Linguistic Papers*, especially pp. 59–64 and 75–81.

Yet one can easily think of occasions on which he might use names of which he has this kind of command for the purpose of identifying reference.

Third, one should notice that a name may sometimes be successfully used, or understood, by one who does not, in either of the ways so far distinguished, know who he means by the name. That is, he need not have either perceptual knowledge or non-name-dependent descriptively identifying knowledge of the bearer of the name. Think, say, of a tutor with a list of freshmen, making teaching arrangements with a colleague.

So it is clear that the formal conditions for the successful use of a name cover a wide range of cases—from the case of minimal identifying knowledge mentioned last up through all degrees of richness of identifying knowledge.

3. REMARK ON A THEORETICAL PROPOSAL FOR ELIMINATING NAMES

Here I would like to interpolate a theoretical remark; or, rather, a remark about a theoretical proposal. If we bear in mind all the considerations we have before us regarding the functioning of ordinary personal names in ordinary human intercourse, we must surely be quite sceptical of that well-known view[2] according to which, without frustration of any essential purpose of the use of names, each name could be 'parsed as', or replaced by, a corresponding unitary predicate which did *not* covertly contain the name on one side of an identity sign. For if we ask what links together all the very various occasions of the referring use of a name for a particular person, the only answer we can give with any confidence is that the name is used on all those occasions to refer to that person.

4. NON-PERSONAL NAME-BEARERS

So far I have talked exclusively about personal names. Now, by way of a check on the course I have followed, I shall briefly consider some other things which do or do not have names. Note that not all I have said about personal names will apply to all personal names. For example, the circumstances of use of names for remoter historical personages obviously differ in possibly significant respects from the circumstances of use of names of contemporary people with whom one has transactions. A complete account of names would have to reckon with these differences. But our aim is not a complete account. We are concerned

[2] Advanced by Quine in many books and articles.

with some central cases and features. So let us now look at some non-personal cases.

Next to persons I mentioned places as obvious bearers of names. By this vague term I meant such things as these: towns, streets, buildings (e.g. theatres, restaurants, churches); geo-political divisions like countries and counties; geographical features like rivers, mountains, seas, bays, capes; and so on. Let us set by the side of this list a fairly random assortment of things which typically do not bear proper names: particular cars, railway carriages, rooms in houses, individual pieces of furniture, articles of clothing, personal objects such as cigarette lighters, spectacles; individual copies of books; individual flowers, trees, insects. Obviously this list could be indefinitely extensive and its items quite heterogeneous.

Does contemplation of these lists force any modification of my original set of basic conditions for the utility of the institution of names? Let us consider some cases. Some non-bearers of names, though they may be of interest as objects of identifying reference within a discourse-group, are only transiently so, e.g. the cigar I am smoking, or one of the flowers I have just arranged. Two circumstances count against names having any utility here. First the circumstances which make them of transient interest will usually be such that they can very easily be identified with the help of the kind-name or even without it: '*your cigar* (is burning the carpet, has gone out)'; '*the yellow one in the middle* (looks incongruous)'. Second, they have to be identified in order for a name for them to be introduced; but, since the interest is transient, the process of identifying which would be necessary for naming, is also sufficient for the short span of identifying interest. Obviously, however, not all objects in the non-name-bearing list are of merely transient interest as objects of identifying reference. I may have the same car, live in the same set of rooms and use the same piece of furniture for years, and often have occasion for identifying reference to these items. But here the other considerations come into play. Within the circle in which there is a standing interest in identifying reference to the object, it is either unique of its kind in being the object of such paramount interest to the members of just that circle—in which case the definite article and kind-name suffice ('the house', 'the car', 'the kitchen' and so on)—or such a fact as that of its ownership, or regular and exclusive use, by one or other member of the circle supplies the salient distinguishing or identifying fact ('my lighter', 'John's room', etc.).

Such objects, then, create no naming-needs. It may be pointed out

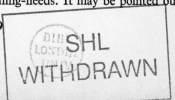

that cars, at least, have registration numbers. But registration numbers differ in important respects from genuine proper names. They are, rather, like the number-labels on the players' backs in my earlier example of the game. The essential thing about them is that they should actually be visibly on the cars, labelling them. They serve primarily as identification marks which thereby generate singular terms with constant descriptive force for referring to the objects which exhibit them. Think of a typical case of their referential utility. A car is observed to knock over a pedestrian at a certain time and place, and go on without stopping. The incident itself supplies us with one definite singular term reflecting a special interest in a certain car: viz. the car which knocked over X at t at p. The problem is to trace or re-identify the car which answers to this description; and if anyone noticed its registration number, then he noticed a mark whereby the car in question can be distinguished from all others when it is remote from the scene of the accident. Then the registration number may be used as a definite singular term for referring to the car. But this sort of use is quite untypical of the use of proper names. Proper names, we might say, owe their referential utility to the complexity or variousness, or both, of their descriptive hinterlands. A registration number emerges into a referential utility only in connection with one particular description: 'the car visibly bearing such-and-such a number'.

Now let us contrast these non-name-bearers with my list of name-bearers, i.e. of places. Of course, as always, we can think of circles and circumstances for which the kind-name with 'the' or 'our' will suffice for identification. The inhabitants of a medieval village in their intercourse with each other may get on very well with 'the church', 'the 'river', 'the bridge' and so on. But people who travel and live in larger communities have more complicated referring needs. It might nevertheless seem difficult to bring the items of the place-list under my statement of general conditions. For surely there *is* one unique fact of salient importance about any such item, viz. its spatial position. This is why I could not unnaturally refer to them all as places. Would not coupling the kind-name with the position give us just what we want without the need for names? But the answer to this is obvious. If one tries giving a spatially locating description for typical items in my list without using any names at all for any such items, it becomes clear why they have names. The only generally available form for a pure, i.e. place-name-free, description of this kind would be that of a description relating the item concerned to some item which could be demonstratively indicated in the setting of the speaker-hearer exchange. Not only would this frequently be complicated and sometimes beyond the speaker's powers. It would defeat the original idea of a single description constantly available within a given circle of referrers. For though the object stays in one position, speakers and hearers do not. So their spatial relations to the object might be different on every different occasion of reference.

Of course there is another way of giving position without explicit relational description and without reliance on names: e.g. by a system of map references, which would yield one standard singular term for a circle using always the same map; or, on a larger scale, by the use of some global coordinate system. Why are the resulting singular terms not names? Is it because they are systematically generated? No! It is not the bare fact that the resulting singular terms are systematically generated that makes them not names; it is the fact that their use, their efficacy, in identifying reference is tied to the system of generation that makes them not names.

I think these cases, then, fall under my broadly stated conditions. One small objection is worth mentioning. It might be objected that I held it against the claim of registration numbers to count as proper names, that they were essentially displayed on their objects. But at least some place-names are typically displayed on *their* objects, e.g. names of restaurants, cinemas and streets. Why do I not reckon this against their claim to count as proper names? One cannot wholly answer this by saying that the point of displaying the name is simply to announce the name to new users, as could be said, perhaps, of those name-labels which people sometimes wear at conferences. For though this may be partly the point, it is not the whole point. The displayed names do also serve as identification marks. But the point is that the names do not serve only as identification marks, and do not serve the purpose of identifying reference only in connection with their serving as identification marks. The name may indeed serve this latter purpose; but its function in identifying reference is not conventionally tied to its doing so. If there were such a tie, the name would be no name.

2. Names and identity
So much, in general, on the command and use of names. By way of transition to theory I now discuss briefly a problem sometimes thought to be raised by identity-statements such as 'Cicero is Tully'. If the statement is true, then one and the same particular item is twice over

identifyingly referred to, the two identifying expressions being linked with such an expression as 'is' or 'was' or 'is/was the same thing/person as' or 'is/was identical with'. How can such a statement be informative? For is not the statement, if true, simply identifying the same thing twice over and saying nothing about it, saying merely that it is itself? And even if it should be easy to see through the difficulty in the case of other identity-statements, does not the difficulty remain acute in the case of identity-statements which couple names, for the very reason that I insisted on earlier in criticizing the proposal to reparse names as general terms? We were to ask what linked together all the multifarious uses and understandings by different speakers and hearers of a name for a given person; what not only linked them together but distinguished them from the use and understanding of names for other persons; and it seemed that the only general answer we could give with any confidence is that the name is used on all these occasions to refer to *that very person*. And of course what goes for one name for a given person goes for any other name for that person. So we might be perplexed for a moment as to how we could understand an identity-statement linking the two names without already knowing it to be true.

The real problem with this problem is to state it without at the same time giving away the solution; or part of the solution. This part of the solution is immediately obvious as soon as we think of the conditions of command of a name. For a hearer of a name to have command of the name, as then used, it is sufficient that the name invoke some kind of identifying knowledge, in the hearer's possession, of the bearer of the name. But of course there is no reason in the world why a hearer should not be in possession of, as it were, segregated bundles or clusters of identifying knowledge which are in fact, unknown to him, bundles or clusters of identifying knowledge about the same thing. If this is so, and if one name in an identity-statement invokes one such cluster, while the other invokes another, then indeed the hearer will learn something, and not simply something about expressions, from the identity-statement which couples the two expressions. (The segregated bundles of identifying knowledge thus brought together and tied up into one for a given audience of an identity-statement may be of different kinds—e.g. a recognitional capacity plus a piece of identifying descriptive knowledge—or of the same kind.)

Now I think it might be said that this answer, though true as far as it goes, misses the point of the problem. This answer shows that different audiences, variously equipped, might learn various different things from one and the same identity statement. It might have different informative values, so to speak, for each of them. But the question is really about the constant informative value, if any, which it has for everyone who learns anything from it. For, after all, we have to do with one and the same proposition; and if that proposition is informative we ought to be able to say what its constant informative value is. Everyone who, having command of the names, learns anything from the proposition that Caesar was bald, or the proposition that Caesar loved Brutus, learns the same things in each case, viz., with respect to that individual, that he was bald, and with respect to the two individuals in question, that the first loved the second. We cannot construct any satisfactory parallel account of what *every one* who learns anything from it learns from the true identity-statement: if we try to construct a parallel, all we get is the non-information that the individual in question is self-identical. And that is the problem again.

How should we react to this? We can accept the pressure of the parallel with ordinary predication, cling to our sense of the informativeness of identity-statements and in desperation say: well, everybody who learns anything from the statement learns at least the empirical fact that the two names, the two expressions, apply to one and the same thing; so it is, properly considered, a statement about expressions. And this view has been held. Again, we can accept the pressure of the parallel, cling to the view that it is not a statement about expressions—for the names are used to refer and not simply to represent themselves—and accept the view that it is, properly understood, non-informative; that, properly understood, it is tautology if true, a self-contradiction if not, though, doubtless a special kind of tautology or contradiction. And then we can enlarge on this view by combining it with an element in the first view: by saying, that is, that though the statement itself is strictly speaking non-informative, yet it is possible to learn from its utterance the empirical fact that the two names apply to the same thing; and this is the common thing which is learnt by anyone who learns from the utterance of the statement.

The intellectual discomfort which we feel in the face of these views is justified; but it is very easy to locate its source in the wrong place; to feel that what we need is a different account of what an identity-statement says, of its content. But this is not what we need. What we need is to resist the pressure of the parallel with ordinary one- or two-place predications; to get a clear enough view of the difference between the statements in question and these ordinary predications. If we get a clear enough view, we see that the problem of giving a general account, valid for all audiences, of the informativeness of a particular statement of the kind concerned can be solved, as it is conspicuously not solved by the views just considered. The mistake is to suppose that the solution must take the same form as it takes for any ordinary predicative proposition.

In the case of any ordinary predicative proposition, we can give a general account, valid for all audiences, of *what* anyone who is informed by that proposition is informed of; whereas in the case of a given identity-statement it does not seem that we can do this. But this does not mean that in the case of a given identity-statement we cannot give a general account, valid for all audiences, of *how* anyone who is informed by that proposition is informed. To be able to do this is to be able to say in what the general informativeness of that proposition consists.

In a sense I have already given the general form of such a general account. But it will help to have a model or picture. Indeed I shall offer two models or pictures. They will be models of the different styles of informativeness of, on the one hand, ordinary predications—one-or-more-place—with names as subjects and, on the other hand, of identity statements coupling two names. The point of the models will be, by bringing out the difference in a sufficiently striking way, to provide us with the means of resisting the pressure of the parallel.

I offer, then, a model or a picture of a man's knowledge of, or belief about, all those particular items of which he has some identifying as well as some non-identifying knowledge. We are to picture a map as it were, of his identifying historical and geographical knowledge—in an extended sense of these words. On the knowledge-map we represent the unity of every cluster of identifying knowledge (i.e. identifying knowledge which the man regards as identifying knowledge of one and the same particular item) by a filled-in circle or dot, such as is used to represent stations on railway maps. Any name he knows which for him in suitable circumstances invokes that cluster of identifying knowledge is written adjacent to the dot. From each dot radiate lines bearing one-or-more-place predicate expressions; and these lines, with their inscriptions, represent the various propositions which the man is able to affirm, from his own knowledge, regarding the items which the appropriate cluster of identifying knowledge is knowledge of. These lines are of different kinds. Some join one dot to another. These are relational propositions like 'Caesar loved Brutus'. Some curl back on their dot of origin. They are reflexively relational propositions like 'Caesar loved himself'. Some are joined to a dot only at one end. These are non-relational propositions like 'Caesar was bald'. Now when a man equipped with such a knowledge-map receives what is for him new information, as audience of a statement containing a name or names which invoke some cluster or clusters of identifying knowledge in his possession, he incorporates such new information in his stock of knowledge. And we may represent his incorporation of this further information into his stock of knowledge by his making an alteration to his knowledge-map. When the statement to which he is audience is an ordinary relational statement, he draws a further line between two dots. When it is a statement ascribing some non-relational property or happening to one of his items, he draws a further line of the kind which terminates in a dot at only one end. But when it is an identity-statement containing two names from which he receives new information, he adds no further lines. He has at least enough lines already; at least enough lines and certainly one too many dots. So what he does is to eliminate one dot of two, at the same time transferring to the remaining one of the two all those lines and names which attach to the eliminated dot and are not already exactly reproduced at the surviving dot. And this gives us a general picture, valid for all audiences who learn from a given identity-statement, of the difference it makes to the knowledge-state of each one of them. It is a *general* picture because in each case—in the map of *every* audience thus informed—the appropriate two name-bearing dots are replaced by one, and the total number of lines reduced by the elimination of duplicates. What we cannot do, of course, is give a detailed specification, valid for all audiences, of what lines are transferred and what eliminated as duplicates. This is what varies from audience to audience.

We might improve this model, perhaps. Instead of thinking of the man as operating on his knowledge-map, when his knowledge-state is changed, we may think simply of the knowledge-map as becoming changed. When he learns something from an ordinary predication, new lines inscribe themselves on his map, attached to the appropriate dot or joining two different dots. When he learns from an identity-statement, the two appropriate dots approach each other and merge, or coalesce, into one, any duplicating lines merging or coalescing at the same time.

The model helps us to see what was troubling us. Our eyes were too firmly fixed on the case of the ordinary predication. So we were inclined to think that the only way in which a statement including a reference already on the map could be informative for all audiences informed by it would be by adding detail, and the same detail, to each of their maps—by adding lines, and the same lines, to each of their maps. But we see there is another way—the same in general for all audiences informed by it—in which an identity-statement can change the knowledge-state of all audiences informed by it.

Here is another model. Imagine a man as, in part, a machine for receiving and storing knowledge of all items of which he already has some identifying knowledge. The machine contains cards, one card for each cluster of identifying knowledge in his possession. On receipt of an ordinary predication invoking one such cluster, the appropriate card is withdrawn, the new information is entered on it and the card is returned to stock. On receipt of an ordinary relational predication invoking two such clusters, the two appropriate cards are withdrawn, cross-referring entries are made on both and both cards are returned to stock. On receipt of an identity-statement invoking two such clusters, the two appropriate cards are withdrawn and a new card is prepared, bearing *both* the names of which one heads one of the original cards and one the other, and incorporating the sum of the information contained in the orginal cards; the single new card is returned to stock and the original cards are thrown away. Here is a simple general procedure of modification of the machine's contents, common to all machines, all audiences, which are informed by the identity-statement. But of course the total number of entries in the machine's stock is not increased; if this number is altered at all, it is diminished, by the elimination of what turn out to be duplicate entries. And of course there is no single general account to be given of the entries summed on to the new card; this will vary from machine to machine.

Of course such models as these have various imperfections. (It might be better to speak of belief-maps or belief-machines rather than of knowledge-maps or knowledge-machines.) Equally certainly they could be improved. But it would be idle to improve them beyond the point at which they fulfil their purpose. Their purpose is to help us to escape from a typically, philosophically obsessive way of looking at our question. Once we are clear, we can relax. We can yield to the pressure for some theoretical assimilation. We can say: yes, such an utterance, if true, is a kind of necessary truth; though, of course, it is not such that, merely in virtue of having command of the names, we automatically know it to have this character.

3. Names in the framework of logic: proper names, variable names and descriptive names

I. PROPER NAMES

Now to edge further towards theory. I have been discussing proper names as they figure in a certain role—call it 'referential'—which is their primary role, in that we understand whatever else they do in the light of their capacity to fill this role. They do not always fill this role. They do not fill it when they are virtually self-quoting, when a bare shade divides 'N' from 'named "N" ': as in that old style of historical opening, 'A certain John Smith, a citizen of Canterbury . . .'; or in the question 'Is there a Mr Robinson here?'; or even in the formula 'This is John Smith', used introducingly of someone of whom the addressee has, and is known to have, no previous knowledge. (The last case is, perhaps, debatable; but one must consider what debates are worthwhile.) There are other secondary styles of name-employment. There is, for example, an interesting area of problems created by the uses, themselves very diverse, of fictional names as such; there are distinctions to be drawn, as between telling a story in the first place, re-telling a story, making a factual claim about an established story. The area merits accurate description; but it really is a secondary area of name-employment and the problems it raises are secondary problems.

What, then, of the primary area and the primary problems? In the assertive utterance of such a sentence as 'John is unwell today', we normally have an assertion of a proposition of our basic class of subject–predicate propositions, with the name 'John', as subject, playing the primary, referential role. That such a sentence can be used successfully in such a way depends, of course, essentially on facts about the social context and setting of its use, on the matter of name-using circles and command of names-as-used. The proposition asserted in uttering the sentence is made available by its utterance only to those who have command of the name-as-then-used. But to them it is made available. In an appropriate setting the name, as used, will *act* as an ideal or Russellian proper name would act if there were such a thing: i.e. as a name which is essentially borne by one and only one thing, and to know the meaning of which is simply to know what thing that is. As far as particulars are concerned, such names are fabled entities. (It could scarcely be an impossibility to give one thing another's name, to name it *after* the other—whatever the other's name.) But there is a kind of sense in the fable. It tries to reproduce, in a context-free style, the character which an ordinary proper name, as used in a social context, has, if all goes well, in that context. One might say, that, in its context of use, the name is *heard as* an ideal name. (One might even say, paradoxically, that the *token*-name *is* an ideal name.) The name used need not always be, as we oddly say, the *real* name of the person referred to, for this to be true; for one has grasp, or command, of the name-as-then-used if one knows who the speaker meant by it.

In making this last remark I can be seen as moving, or shifting, in a certain 'theoretical' direction. In general when we talk of 'theories' in this area, 'theories' of reference and so forth, we are nowadays often talking of different choices that might be made of ways of fitting onto each other, or bringing into relation to each other, two kinds of thing: on the one hand, the complex phenomena of actual discourse, all that is done, and the background to what is done, when we talk to each other; on the other, some relatively simple paradigm or framework, such as that provided by our logic. If I now press ahead with one way of doing this, without much immediate consideration of other possibilities, this implies no denial that there are workable alternatives which will have a greater appeal for some.

One theoretically central, though practically peripheral, question runs as follows. What of the very rare but not impossible case where there is an intended primary use of a name but nothing whatever could count as grasp, or command, of the name as then used (or even mis-used)? A primary use is intended; but there just does not exist any real particular such that to indicate or specify that particular would be correctly to answer the question, 'Who/what is being named (or even mis-named) by the name?' Such a situation could arise, for example, in certain cases of fraud, when the innocent and deceived might take themselves to be using a name in the primary way in assertive communications with each other, but be completely mistaken in this. The answer I suggest is simple. If there is nothing which counts as command-of-the-name-as-then-used, then there is no proposition asserted, though the speaker by hypothesis thinks there is. Consequently there is no true or false proposition asserted. But there is no neither-true-nor-false proposition asserted either. It is not necessary to eliminate names in order to prevent truth-value-gaps from opening.

Given, then, a putative utterance of a proposition of our basic class with, say, a personal name in the '*a*' place, we have it that a necessary condition of such a proposition being expressed by the utterance is that there should actually exist someone to whom the speaker is referring in uttering the name, that the name in his mouth on that occasion refers to someone real. But what exactly settles this question, the question whether there actually exists someone to whom the speaker is referring in using the name? Again the principle is simple. Once the speaker becomes *fully informed of relevant matters*, it is for him to say. His (sincere) answer settles the question: it settles not only the question whether there was anyone, but the question who, if anyone, it was. Relevant information will be of the form: there exists just one thing answering to all of *these* descriptions, there does not exist anything answering to all of *these*. Enough of such information, suitably chosen, will leave the speaker in no doubt. He will be able to say: Yes, in the light of this information, I can definitely say that there does (as I supposed) exist someone to whom I was referring in using the name; or: No, in the light of this information, I am bound to admit that there does not exist anyone to whom I was referring in using the name. In the first case, the speaker was indeed propounding such a proposition as he took himself to be propounding, in the second case he was not. Relevant matters may, of course, be different matters for different speakers even when all of them are using the same name with the same actual reference; and the quickest way of eliciting the confirming 'Yes' from all of them might be to make very different selections, for each of them, from the available mass of information. This merely reflects facts already dwelt on about the conditions of command of names. Different name-users may all have achieved command of the same name for the same item, and hence be in a position to express a proposition about that item by the use of the name, even though they have achieved command of the name in very different ways. The relevant necessary condition of the proposition expressed by one being the proposition understood by another is simply that the item the speaker refers to and the item the audience takes the speaker to refer to be identical.

So long as we understand what in principle settles the question whether anyone who utters a *sentence* of the appropriate form expresses a *proposition* of that form at all; and also what settles the question, granted that he expressed such a proposition, *who* or *what* he refers to by the name (or names); then that is all we need. There is nothing more to be understood.[3]

[3] Recent discussion makes it worth adding this: any reflective speaker will acknowledge that he cannot have *meant* a particular item by the use of a name on a particular occasion unless he had *some* identifying *knowledge* of that item; and he could not (in general) have acquired such knowledge save by a *causal* route originating in some fact about the particular concerned.

But I must repeat that there are other ways—some of which I shall shortly mention—of arranging for the facts to live in the frame of logic.[4]

2. VARIABLE AND DESCRIPTIVE NAMES

Since a proper name, in a primary use, is a model or paradigm case of a logical subject-expression in a proposition of our basic class, I shall extend the use of the word 'name' and apply it, with suitable qualification, to other types of expression where they are playing the subject-role. Singular pronouns, where they fill this role, might reasonably be called 'systematically variable names', or, for short, 'variable names'. (Ordinary proper names, like 'John' and 'Peter', regarded as parts of the language, as English names, are really variable names too, only not systematically variable. The conventions that make them available for use in the primary role, as referring now to this person, now to that, are not conventions of the language, but *ad hoc* or local or special name-using-circle conventions.)

It is frequently pointed out that singular pronouns often function like bound variables of quantification; and then of course there is no question of regarding them as playing their other role, that of variable names. They *can* be variables; and they *can* be variable names, fill the logical-subject role. When they function as variable names, the situation is not so very different from that of the use of ordinary proper names in their primary role. The proposition asserted in uttering the sentence containing the variable name is made available by its utterance only to those who have grasp of the variable-name-as-then-used: i.e. who know who or what is meant by its use. Of course the conventions which help us to a grasp of the variable name as used are different from the local or special proper-name-using conventions on which we in part rely in order to know who a speaker means, in a given setting, by 'John' or 'Jean'. There is more than one source of grasp of the variable name.

[4] The question may be raised of the status, on any such view as the above, of utterances of existential sentences containing names, e.g. of such sentences as 'Caesar exists'. The answer should be evident: the character of the utterance depends on the way in which the name is used in making it. If the name is *not* used in the primary, referential way, utterance of such a sentence could be the expression of a true, or of a false, proposition: a proposition to the effect, say, that there does exist someone whom we (the relevant group) are talking about when we use the name 'Caesar' with a primary name-using intention. If, on the other hand, the name *is* used, in the utterance of the affirmative existential sentence, with a primary, referential intention, then the utterance of the sentence could fail to express a proposition at all; but if it expresses a proposition at all, then it can only express a true one. What is ruled out in this case is that it expresses a false proposition.

Somebody goes out of a room; and somebody says: 'He seemed a bit upset'. We know who is meant. 'He' functions here just as well as an ideal name would function if there were such a thing and if we knew it was the, or a, name of the man who had just gone out. Or again—a quite different case—we often begin by using names and then, later in the same narrative or report, use pronouns instead. Thus: 'John is unwell today. He drank too much yesterday.' Here *linguistic* context enters into, contributes to, grasp of the variable name, as it does not in the first case. Our grasp of the variable name depends on our independent grasp, if we have such a grasp, of the name 'John' as then used.

As in the case of the intended primary use of proper names, it may, on rare occasions, happen that someone intends to assert a proposition of our basic class, using a pronoun as a variable name, in a case where nothing would in fact count as grasp of the name as then used. Then, once more, he does not assert a false proposition or a proposition neither true nor false. He asserts no proposition.

What, now, of definite descriptions? (We construe the expression widely enough to include phrases with a manifestly token-reflexive element, such as 'that chair' or 'your brother'.) Do they ever function as names, i.e. as logical subject-expressions? If, and in so far as, they do, they will clearly be a different class of names from proper names or variable (or pronominal) names; we might have ready for them the title 'descriptive names', or, perhaps, 'improper names'.

To say that descriptions may sometimes function as descriptive names will not of course be to say that they always function so, any more than to say that pronouns sometimes function as variable names is to say that they always function so. It may be that sometimes descriptions function as descriptive names and sometimes more after the pattern of a Russellian analysis. From the fact that expressions share a recognizable English structure, it does not follow that all of them, in all their occurrences, are best fitted in the same way into the frame of logic. So what follows is not a general account of definite descriptions. It is an account —or a contribution to an account—of definite descriptions functioning as descriptive names.

If we acknowledge descriptive names, our principal problem will be to give an account of the way in which the conventional sense of the description bears on its functioning as a descriptive name.

Two test-cases for any such account are: (a) the case in which the sincere speaker, on being fully informed, acknowledges that contrary to his belief at the time of speaking, there exists in fact no item at all such that he intended to refer to that item by the use of the descriptive name; (b) the case in which there does exist such an item, but the description contained in the descriptive name does not apply to it. In case (a) there exists no individual at all which or whom the speaker *meant*; in case (b) the individual the speaker meant does not answer to the description which he used of it.

I consider three possible accounts of these cases. The first two accounts agree in their verdicts on case (a), but differ in their verdicts on case (b). They agree that in case (a) the speaker—supposing that he intends, say, to *assert* his proposition—in fact asserts no proposition; for nothing counts as grasp of the descriptive name he used, as he used it. The accounts differ as to whether or not the speaker asserts a proposition in case (b). According to account (1), the speaker does assert a proposition in case (b) and the truth or falsity of the proposition is determined solely by whether the predicate of the proposition is truly or falsely predicable of the item which the speaker meant by his descriptive name. According to account (2), the speaker does not succeed in asserting a proposition in case (b); for a proposition to be asserted it is required not only that there should be some item to which the speaker intended to refer, but also that the description he uses should apply to that item.

If we adopt account (2), we might feel in consistency bound to stiffen our requirements for the assertion of a proposition in the case of proper names and variable names as well: to insist that a proper name used to refer to an item be 'really' one of its names, that something referred to as 'he' be male etc., as a condition of allowing that a proposition is asserted by one who refers, or attempts to refer, in such terms.

The descriptions of cases (a) and (b) alike leave open a possibility not so far mentioned: the possibility that though there exists no item which both answers to the description used and is the intended object of the speaker's reference, yet there does exist an item of which it is true both that the description contained in the descriptive name applies to that item and that in the social and physical context of the speaker's utterance it would be reasonable and natural to take it that a speaker, speaking conventionally in that context, would mean (intend to refer to) that item. Our third account—account (3)—differs from the previous two in holding that in such a case the speaker has in fact referred to *this* item and asserted a proposition about *it*, though it was no part of his intention to do so; and that the proposition he has asserted is true or false according as its predicate is truly or falsely predicable of this item.

Account (3) is not completely developed. But of the three accounts as we have them, it is clear that account (1) is that which gives the most weight to the intention of the speaker and the least to the descriptive content of the description he uses, and account (3) that which gives the most weight to the conventional sense of the description and the least to the speaker's intention, account (2) falling between them in these respects. Even on account (1), the conventional sense of the description is not otiose; for it will normally be, and will be intended to be, an important part of the means whereby the audience is brought to understand what item the speaker is referring to, and, hence, what proposition he is asserting (or otherwise propounding). And even on account (3), it is by no means the case that the speaker's intention is a theoretical irrelevance; for though, on account (3), a speaker's actual reference may not be intended by him, yet the criteria of actual reference are explained in terms of the concept of intended reference. Moreover, it would seem not to be inconsistent either with the letter or with the spirit of account (3) as we have it, to develop it, for a sub-case which it does not so far explicitly cover, with the following rule: where (i) there is an item which the speaker intends to refer to and that item answers to the description he uses, and (ii) there is also an item which answers to that description and of which it is true that in the social and physical context of the speaker's utterance it would be reasonable and natural to take it that a speaker, speaking conventionally in that context, would mean that item, and (iii) these items are not identical, then it is the first item and not the second which the proposition asserted by the speaker is about; so that, in such a case, it is to be what the speaker actually *meant*, rather that what he would normally be taken to mean, that governs the ruling on what he *said*.

How should account (3) be developed for the case in which, though there exists an item which the speaker intends to refer to, that item does not answer to the description used, and there exists no item which both answers to the description used and is such that it would be reasonable and natural to take it that a speaker, speaking in that context, would mean that item? In such cases it would seem consistent with the spirit of account (3) as we have it, to join forces with account (2) rather than account (1): i.e. to require, as the condition of a speaker's having asserted a proposition, that the item which the speaker intends to refer to should answer to the description used.

If we adopt account (3) we might feel in consistency bound to revise correspondingly our earlier theoretical account of the conditions of the assertion of a proposition, and of the identity of the proposition, if any, which is asserted, in the cases of proper names and variable names (pronouns). It is obvious how the revision should go, so I will not set it out.

There is another consideration with which we can supplement the accounts before us in such a way as to do, perhaps, fuller justice to the conventional sense of a description when it is employed as a descriptive name. On any of these three accounts it remains an open possibility that a speaker who so employs a description yet fails to assert a proposition: on the first account because there may not exist in fact any item such that the speaker intends to refer to that item; on the second account because it may be that even though there exists such an item, it does not answer to the description employed; and on the third account because there may exist no item which either both answers to the description and is meant by the speaker or both answers to the description and is such that a conventional speaker could reasonably be taken, in the context, to mean it. However, on any account, the fact that a speaker, speaking seriously, uses as a descriptive name the description he does so use, with the conventional sense which it has, shows him as committed to the belief that there exists *some* item answering to that description. (He is committed, indeed, to more than this; but he is committed to at least this.) We can say, then, that his use of the words he does use carries with it a commitment to the truth of a proposition to the effect that there exists some item of a certain kind, the kind in question being determined by the conventional sense of the words of his description. Now the proposition of this existential form to which the speaker is thus committed cannot, on any of our three views, be happily described as a logical part of, or included in, what he actually says (e.g. asserts). For the commitment to this existential proposition is a commitment which holds quite irrespective of whether the speaker succeeds in asserting a proposition or not; and from the extreme supposition that the existential proposition to which the speaker is in this way committed was false, there would, on none of the three accounts, follow the consequence that he had asserted any false proposition. On the contrary, on the second and third accounts, it would follow that he had failed to assert a proposition at all; while on the first account the supposition would be consistent with the possibility that he had asserted a true proposition (and also with the possibilities that he had asserted a false proposition or no proposition).

The topic of commitments not included in the content of the proposition, if any, which the speaker asserts (or which he propounds in any other intended mode) could be pursued further. But let this suffice.

It is a natural, and justifiable, reaction to the three accounts we have before us to say that none of them is wholly satisfactory. Should we conclude that our failure is simply a failure of ingenuity, that with a little more patience and skill we should surely hit on a way of fitting descriptive names into the frame of logic, which would be wholly satisfactory, which would be the correct way of doing so? Or should we conclude rather, that no attempt should be made to distinguish some occurrences of definite descriptions as descriptive names or logical subject expressions, and that the only acceptable way of fitting definite descriptions into the frame of logic is to treat them all alike on the general pattern of Russell's original analysis?

Both these conclusions would be mistaken, and the mistake is a mistake of principle. The mistake is to think that there must always be just one correct way of fitting the facts of discourse into the framework of logic. Our immediate concern has been with a certain not very sharply defined range of occurrences (occurrences as 'descriptive names') of expressions of a certain recognizable English structure ('definite descriptions'). It is possible to describe a wide variety of cases of the use of expressions of this structure. Some of these cases will fall clearly within the range we are concerned with, some will fall clearly outside it, some will be borderline cases. Our case-descriptions, taking account of linguistic features and psychological, social and physical circumstances, could be quite realistic, literally true and full enough to neglect no relevant factor. Yet from such full and literal descriptions of cases we cannot simply deduce the correct way of fitting each utterance into the frame of logic. We are left with decisions to make.

Logical theory presents us with boldly distinguished, sharply contrasted possibilities of classification for all the cases we might thus laboriously describe. For a given case, fully described, we are required, perhaps, to choose between: 'true proposition', 'false proposition', 'no proposition'; to choose between conflicting identifications of what was asserted (or otherwise propounded) by the speaker. What controls are there on the realism of our responses? The ordinary use of the expressions 'true', 'false', 'what he said' in these cases may simply not be definite enough to supply us with controls. We hesitate: or we say, now one thing, now another. Any choice, among those open to us, may seem to involve some distortion, some forcing of the facts, some artificiality. Wittgenstein is reported to have said that in logic all differences are big differences. That is a part of the trouble. For our laborious descriptions may present us with a range of cases between which there are small gradations of difference.

So there is no wholly realistic way of fitting *all* the facts into the framework of logic. There is nothing to deplore in this. To think that there was, to resist this conclusion *à outrance*, would be to misunderstand the character both of logic and of common discourse. The lack of perfect fit between them is not an imperfection in either.

Where perfect fit is impossible, and we yet persist with our question, what considerations should determine our choice of answer? It is easy to say: choose the answer which involves least distortion of the facts. This is like saying: give most weight to the weightiest considerations. There is no commonly accepted scale. Yet in providing, in one way or another, for definite descriptions to figure, in some cases, as logical subject expressions, we are surely giving weight to considerations to which weight should be given. As we saw in our earlier discussion of proper names of particular persons or places, names are but one device for performing a basic function in linguistic communication, viz. that of identifying reference to such items; and this function can sometimes be performed as naturally and easily, and sometimes more naturally and easily, by the use of short definite descriptions. Obsessed by the cases where things go wrong, we pay too little attention to the vastly more numerous cases where they go right, and where it is perhaps easier to see that the descriptive content of the expression concerned is wholly at the service of this function, a function which is complementary to that of predication and contains no element of predication in itself. This is the case for assimilating descriptions, so used, to what logic recognizes as names.

The facts behind the assimilation, however, are more important than the assimilation itself or the details of the form it may take. If we can find no form which wholly satisfies us, we should not, I repeat, be distressed. The simplifications of logic may greatly help us to understand the complexities of discourse; but we should not allow our understanding to be trammelled by those simplifications.

4. General names

A proposal has been made for extending the application of the notion of a subject-term or logical name in a quite different direction from any so far considered. The proposal has not been formally worked out and I shall argue that no sufficient case has been made for attempting to work it out. Yet there is advantage to be gained from discussing it. Even if it points to no interesting grammar of logic, yet it may have a bearing on grammar more widely conceived.

The subject-terms we have so far discussed—the replacements for the 'a's and 'b's in 'Fa', 'Fab', etc.—are essentially *singular* terms. In the basic cases, each specifies or identifies a single particular, in the non-basic cases each specifies or identifies a single non-particular. One famous proposal, Quine's, is that all such terms should be swept away from the ideal logical language, leaving no singular terms but variables. The proposal we are now to consider has exactly the opposite tendency: the logical category of names, or subject-terms, should be extended to include some non-singular terms, some general names.[5]

I can best introduce the proposal with the help of an example. Consider the general proposition of ordinary English 'All elephants are playful'. The orthodox mode of representing the proposition in our current logic is '(x) (if x is an elephant, then x is playful)'. In this representation there is nothing which can be counted as a subject-term, subject-position is occupied by variables and the expressions 'elephant' and 'playful' both appear in predicate-position. According to the proposal we are to consider, the general proposition in question is not best represented in this way. It is better viewed as containing or consisting of (1) a subject-term, viz. 'elephants', which does not specify a *single* item of any sort, and (2) a predicate-term, viz, 'All . . . are playful'. (It need hardly be said that the expressions 'subject' and 'predicate', as so employed, are not to be confused with their counterparts in the traditional logic of the syllogism. The quantifier 'all', for example, is here proposed as part of the predicate-term, whereas in the traditional representation it would form part of neither subject nor predicate.)

Clearly we have here a departure in the use of the terms 'subject' and 'predicate'; and we should have at least drastically to modify the notions of subject and predicate, and the structure of our logical theory, in order to accommodate the extension of the terms in this direction. I

---

[5] I have derived this proposal entirely from the writings of Geach (see *Reference and Generality*, Chapters 2 and 7, and *Logic Matters*, especially 1.5); but since I do not wish to saddle him with a responsibility, which he might not welcome or acknowledge, for the way in which I shall interpret it, I shall speak impersonally of 'the proposal', 'the advocate of the proposal', etc.

The examples I give all involve universal quantification. This secures some economy in expression, but does not, I think, limit the principle of the discussion, which could easily be extended to cover any case the proposal is intended to cover.

shall not discuss the question whether such a modification could be easily or effectively performed, but, rather some reasons why it might be thought worth attempting.

To find these reasons we must look for relevant reasons for rejecting the orthodox representation of the form of the generalization. I think one set of reasons consists in a view which might be roughly expressed as follows: we understand the generalization correctly only if we see it as a generalization of singular subject–predicate propositions *about elephants*; but the orthodox form of representation prevents our seeing it in this way and encourages us instead to assimilate it to a class of general propositions to which it does not really belong.

Now to try to put this more clearly. Consider the class of standard (i.e. singular) subject–predicate propositions of which the subjects refer identifyingly to particular elephants, identified *as* particular *elephants*, and of which the common predicate is 'is playful'. What does this phrase, 'identified as particular elephants', mean? If we accept either the second or the third account, given above, of descriptive names, then the answer is clear in cases in which the subject-term (of a proposition of which the predicate is 'is playful') is such an expression as 'this elephant' or 'that elephant'. Where the subject-term is a proper name, say 'Ranee', or 'Rajah', the answer is less clear. But suppose it were *de facto* the case that whenever such an elephant-name was used in the primary way, and a proposition was thereby successfully propounded, every speaker or hearer who knew what *creature* was referred to also understood the name as the name of an *elephant*. The supposition does not seem very extravagant. It would allow us to include all propositions of which the subject-terms refer, by name, to particular elephants in the class we are concerned with. Let us call this class of propositions the class K_0.

Next consider a different class of propositions. Propositions of this class are formed, by conditional compounding, out of pairs of standard subject–predicate propositions with a common subject-term, the first member of the pair having as predicate 'is an elephant' and the second member of the pair having as predicate 'is playful'. No restriction beyond that of ordinary well-formedness, however, is to be understood as applying to the common subject-term of any such pair. In other words, this class consists of all propositions whatever of the form

if x is an elephant, then x is playful.

Call this class of propositions the class K_1; and add to it the class K_2, which is the class of all subject–predicate propositions of the form

x is, if an elephant, then playful,

where 'if an elephant, then playful' is a compound predicate-expression and, once again, there is no restriction on the range of subject-terms.

Evidently the class K_0 of propositions is quite a different class from the classes K_1 and K_2. For one thing, the subject of any proposition of K_0 is always a term which refers to an elephant, whereas the subject of a proposition of K_2 or the common subject of the constituent propositions of a proposition of K_1 is not required to be such a term. Then there is the further, and connected, difference that the expression 'elephant' figures in the predicate both of K_2 propositions and of the constituent propositions of K_1 propositions, but it has no place in the predicate of K_0 propositions.

Consequently the proposition (P_0) that all the propositions of K_0 are true is quite a different proposition from the proposition (P_1) that all the propositions of K_1 are true or the proposition (P_2) that all the propositions of K_2 are true. No doubt P_0 could not be true without P_1 and P_2 being true as well and conversely.[6] Nevertheless P_0 remains a quite different proposition from P_1 and P_2; for it relates to K_0, a quite different class of propositions from the classes (K_1 and K_2) which P_1 and P_2 respectively relate to, and a class, moreover, which differs much more from K_1 and K_2 than they differ from each other.

Now the proposition

(x) (if x is an elephant, then x is playful)

stands in a certain relation to the proposition P_1 which I shall not try to describe but shall name by saying that '(x) (if x is an elephant, then x is playful)' is the first-order generalization corresponding to P_1. The proposition

(x) (x is, if an elephant, then playful)

stands in this same relation to P_2. I think the view we are considering might be expressed as the view that the proposition

All elephants are playful

should be seen as standing to the proposition P_0 in much the same

---

[6] We suppose P_0, P_1 and P_2 themselves to share a common standard logical form.

relation as the propositions just mentioned stand to P_1 and P_2 respectively; and that to the very great difference we found between P_0 on the one hand and P_1 and P_2 on the other there answers an equally great difference between their corresponding first-order generalizations.

The aim of the proposal, then, is to keep bright the vision of our general proposition as intimately related to, as essentially a generalization of, or from, members of a set of singular subject–predicate propositions of each of which the subject-term is understood as referring to an elephant, identified as such, and in none of which is the concept, *elephant*, presented by a predicate-term. This vision is dimmed if we adopt a mode of representation for our general proposition in which the concept *elephant* is presented by a term in predicate-position; for this mode of representation encourages us rather to think of our general proposition as intimately related to singular propositions in which likewise the concept *elephant* is presented by a term in predicate-position.

Whatever persuasiveness we may find in these considerations, I think the proposal they are designed to elucidate and support can reasonably be resisted as a proposal for logic. The proposal, as argued for, clearly relates not to all general propositions without exception, but to a certain sub-class of them. But there is no clear and general way of distinguishing general propositions which belong to this class from those which do not. (Of course, even if there were a method of making such a division, it would not follow that the motives for making it would outweigh the motives for disregarding it; for a governing consideration in elaborating a logical theory is simplicity and generality in choice of forms for exhibiting logical relationships.)

To make the point good, let us consider some examples:

> All lovers interest the gods
> All poets are sensitive to criticism
> All footballers are beer-drinkers.

Are there, in the case of these propositions, such motives for casting 'lovers', 'poets' and 'footballers' for the role of subject-term as the advocate of our proposal was assumed to have for casting 'elephants' for the role of subject-term of 'All elephants are playful'? It seems unlikely that the advocate of the proposal would find such motives for such a recommendation in these cases. Suppose we were to press the question what singular subject–predicate propositions, if any, were to be thought of as having to these generalizations an analogous relation to that which the propositions of K_0 were said to have to the generalization 'All elephants are playful'. The most plausible answer would seem to be that, in so far as there was an analogous relation of the generalization to singular subject–predicate propositions in these cases, it would be a relation, in each case, to *two* sets of singular subject–predicate propositions; and that these propositions would be such that the term 'lover' would be a part of the *predicate* of each proposition of one set, and such that the term 'interests the gods' would be the *predicate* of each proposition of the other set. Thus items from our sets of propositions might be:

> Dick is a lover
> Tom is a lover
> etc.

from the first set, and

> Dick interests the gods
> Tom interests the gods
> etc.

from the second set. If we then asked what *was* the peculiarly intimate relation of the generalization to the propositions belonging to these sets, the reply might be that the generalization was the first-order generalization corresponding to the proposition that for every true proposition belonging to the first set there was a corresponding true proposition (i.e. a true proposition with the same subject) belonging to the second set. This would be quite a reasonable account to give. But of course such an account as this provides no basis whatever for objecting to the conventional modern representation of the generalization on the ground that it involves introducing the concept, *lover*, by a term in predicate-position. On the contrary, the account supplies an endorsement of this feature of the current logical mode of representation of the generalization.

A defender of the proposal would presumably be prepared to accept this point. He might even be prepared to accept it with alacrity, as suggesting a test whereby the class of generalizations for which his position is intended to hold might be distinguished from the class of generalizations for which it is not intended to hold and of which these examples are instances of a sub-class. For we can, naturally, and quite without strain, rephrase the latter generalizations in such a way that the concepts presented by their *grammatical* subjects are presented instead by terms in predicate-position in relative clauses. Thus for the first we can have the paraphrase, 'All who are lovers interest the gods' or the paraphrase, 'Anyone who is in love interests the gods'. Similarly we can have 'All who are poets . . .', 'Anyone who is a poet . . .', 'Everyone who writes poetry . . .', etc. and 'All who play football . . .', 'Everyone who plays football . . .', etc. No such natural and unstrained form of paraphrase is possible, however, for 'All elephants are playful'. We can indeed write or say the words 'All creatures which are elephants are playful' or 'Every creature which is an elephant is playful', and expect to be understood. But there is a sense of strain about this which is quite absent in the other cases. Here, it might be suggested, we have an intuitive indication, though, to be sure, one which needs a backing of explanatory theory, as to where the line is to be drawn.

These are flimsy defences. Whatever strain we find in 'All creatures which are elephants are playful' as a paraphrase of 'All elephants are playful' we find also in 'All creatures which are terriers [*or* All dogs which are terriers] are playful' as a paraphrase of 'All terriers are playful' and in 'All crustaceans which are lobsters turn red in the boiling' as a paraphrase of 'All lobsters turn red in the boiling'. Should we then regard 'All terriers are playful' as related in the peculiarly intimate way we have discussed to just *one* set of singular subject–predicate propositions ('Tom is playful', 'The terrier is playful', etc.) of which it is supposed true that anyone who grasps the reference of the subject-term identifies what it refers to as a terrier? Or should the generalization be regarded as so related to *two* sets, one consisting of propositions like 'Jim is a terrier' and the other of propositions like 'Jim is playful', regarding which no such suppositions are made? Philosophical dog-fanciers might return one answer, the dog-indifferent another.

We lack a clear general principle in accordance with which we could apply a formal distinction among general propositions such as the proposal requires. This is not to say that the proposal is quite absurd or indefensible. But it is reasonable to resist it as a proposal for a logical theory, partly because there would be a fairly large element of arbitrariness in deciding to allot one general noun to subject-position, another to predicate-position, and partly because any gains in insight which the proposal might be thought to offer would be likely to be more than offset by losses in simplicity and generality of mode of representation. Yet a thought which has some kinship with the thought underlying this proposal may be of some service in our further study of grammar.

Part Two

The Subject in General

3
Language-Types
and
Perspicuous Grammars

In Part One I treated of a notion of subject and predicate associated with the grammar of current logic. In this second part, I first describe a certain general idea of grammar and then, in the light of it, I try gradually to develop another notion of subject and predicate which is different from, and, in a sense, more comprehensive than, the first. I shall not claim that this second conception corresponds exactly with any employed in present or past grammatical theory, nor shall I try to relate that 'certain general idea of grammar' of which I speak to current discussions. My procedure will be thoroughly non-empirical in that I shall not be directly studying actual natural languages—though I shall refer to them for illustrative purposes—but imagined or model languages. Nevertheless the procedure will, I hope, yield some gain in understanding of some general features of some actual languages.

1. Essential grammar and variable grammar

I begin by introducing the notion of a perspicuous grammar. A perspicuous grammar of a language is one in which the actual formal syntactical arrangements of the language are presented as realizations of the *essential* grammar of the *language-type* to which the language belongs. The essential grammar of the language-type is a set of requirements that rules must satisfy rather than an actual set of rules. It stands in necessary connection with the specification of the language-type. The language-type is specified by specifying (1) the semantic types of significant elements which any language of the type contains and (2) the types of semantically functional combination which these elements may enter into to form sentences or to form sentence-parts which themselves enter into such combinations to form sentences. In the bare specification of the language-type no mention is made of any formal arrangements at all by which these semantically significant combinations are represented. The mention of such formal arrangements belongs to the specification of some mode of realization of the essential grammar of a language-type, i.e. to the specification of a *variable* grammar for some possible language or languages of that type.

So a perspicuous grammar for an imagined, or model, language can be designed in four stages. The first stage is the specification of the language-type. The second stage is the deduction of its essential grammar, i.e. of the requirements that must somehow or other be satisfied, or at least satisfied to some reasonable degree, if sentences of a language of the type concerned are to permit of syntactically unambiguous interpretation or at least are not to admit of more than a tolerable measure of syntactic ambiguity. The third stage consists in considering, and choosing among, different possible ways in which these requirements might be satisfied, or at least satisfied to a reasonable degree, i.e. in considering, and choosing among, different possible variable (or *idiosyncratic* or *alternative*) grammars for languages of the given language-type. It is only at this stage, and not before, that the question of actual formal arrangements arises. Finally, at the fourth stage, we may, if we like, set out the rules of a chosen variable grammar systematically, i.e. write a systematic grammar for a language of our language-type. The result will be a *perspicuous* grammar in that there is a guaranteed connection, clearly understood, between formal syntactic features, relations and classifications on the one hand and semantic interpretation on the other.

Though the point is obvious enough, it may be worth remarking parenthetically that this scheme leaves open the theoretical possibility of a plurality of languages of the same language-type differing from each other in a variety of ways. Thus one theoretical possibility is that of two languages which differ only in respect of the phonetic and typographical forms of their elements, so that exact and word-by-word translation is possible from one language to the other. Or again, two languages might differ both in the first way mentioned and also in having different variable grammars, but in no other way at all. Here would be a case in which exact translation was always possible from one language to the other, but not word-by-word translation. And of course there are other, and more realistic, possibilities of difference within the same language-type.

The procedure I outlined for arriving at perspicuous grammars is obviously of a markedly *a priori* character. A natural way of conducting such an exercise would evidently be to start with very simple language-types and progressively to enrich them. Enrichment need not consist only in adding new types of element and new types of permitted functional combination to those already recognized in earlier models. It may consist, in part, of presenting already recognized kinds of combination as special cases of more general kinds newly recognized; and it may consist in providing that significant elements of a certain type (or indeed combinations of elements) may perform semantico-syntactic roles, enter into types of combination, which have not, in previous models, been open to them. And it may be that we have here a feature which is more than a convenience in the conduct of an *a priori* exercise. For it may be that we shall best understand our actual languages by thinking sometimes in terms of derived or secondary semantico-syntactic roles, and by thinking of certain general semantico-syntactic functions as modelled on more primitive special cases of them: two thoughts which may go together in some cases.

With this last sentence I strike a note which must be struck sooner or later. For whatever the intrinsic interest of the *a priori* exercise I sketch, if it is to have a place in the studies which concern us, it must eventually cast light on the structure of actual languages. The hope that it might do so seems not unreasonable. For, on the one hand, it seems reasonable to hold that it should be possible in principle to construct a perspicuous grammar for any actual language. And, on the other hand, in conducting any *a priori* exercise such as I sketch, we shall obviously obtain our materials—our types of element and combination, our types of formal arrangement—by drawing on resources supplied or suggested by the language, or languages, which we know. Of course, in imagining our ideally simplified language-types, we shall draw on these resources in a highly selective way; indeed, especially at first, in a quite unrealistically restrictive way. The advantages of this are that we shall have a clear view of the necessities of essential grammar, and the possibilities of variable grammar, for our constructed language-types. We can have sharp distinctions where natural language offers us only fuzzy boundaries; we need take on no more complexities at any moment than we are ready for. The disadvantages, of course, are complementary: the greater the simplicity and clarity of our constructions, the more remote they will be from the facts. Still, if we have luck in our selections, some of the features which will stand out clearly in our *a priori* sketches may correspond to features characteristic of large groups of natural languages, or even of human languages in general.

There are two levels at which features with the last-mentioned trait—universals of language—might appear in our sketches. The first level is that of the preliminary specification of a language-type. This, I said, consisted in specifying the semantic types of element which any language of the type would contain and the types of functional combination which such elements could enter into to form sentences, or to form sentence-parts themselves capable of entering into such combinations. By an 'element' I mean a semantically significant item of which the significance is not the outcome of syntactic combination of semantically significant parts. The notion of an element must be sufficiently abstract to allow at least of the possibility of the *same* item having variant forms as it appears in different combinations or in different semantico-syntactic roles. As to semantic types of elements: elements which were proper names of individual continuant particulars or substances might form one such type; expressions signifying general kinds of such particulars might form another, and expressions signifying general qualities of such particulars a third. (Here is one point at which, in our imagined or model language-types, we can give our classifications a sharpness not reflected in natural language.) Evidently one semantic type might be included in another, and we shall make only such subdivisions of types as are necessary for the programme in hand at any stage of its development. As to modes of functional combination: the specification of these, as a part of the specification of the language-type concerned, does not, I repeat, involve any reference to formal syntactical arrangements; it consists rather in specifying the semantic character of the outcome of a mode of combination and specifying the functions, relative to each other and to the outcome, of the parts which enter into the combination.

How might universals of language appear at this level in our *a priori* sketches? The answer is obvious. For it might simply be in fact the case that certain semantic types of element are universal features of human languages; and it might simply be in fact the case that certain types of semantico-syntactic combination, in the sense of the phrase I have just indicated, are universal features of human languages. If there are indeed any types of element or combination which are universal features of human languages, the chances of their being mentioned in such *a priori* sketches as I speak of would seem to be reasonably good and to become better in proportion as the sketches are elaborated; especially if the sketches are consciously directed towards reflecting salient characteristics of the semantically expressive powers of a wide range of languages.

I said that there was another level at which universals of language might appear in our *a priori* sketches. And here I have in mind the level at which we consider formal arrangements as realizations of the requirements of the essential grammar of a language-type. Of course it follows from what I have just said about types of element and of combination, that there may be some requirements of *essential* grammar which are universal features of human languages; i.e. that all human languages belong to language-types such that certain requirements of essential grammar are common to all those language-types. But this is not what I now have in mind. What I have in mind is the thought that it might be in fact the case, for *some* requirements of essential grammar and for *some* features of possible formal arrangements for realizing these requirements, that all languages of types which shared these requirements also shared these features of their formal realization. This possibility seems to be theoretically open both for requirements of essential grammar which are themselves universal, if there are any such, and for requirements of essential grammar which are not themselves universal. If this possibility were realized, one could speak of universal features of *variable* grammar, bearing in mind, however, that to call a feature of variable grammar universal would not be to say that it was found in all languages, but only to say that it was found in all languages belonging to types which shared a certain requirement of essential grammar; though these indeed might be all languages.

The two levels I had in mind, then, at which universal features of human language might appear in our *a priori* sketches are the level of specification of a language-type and the level of consideration of the possible formal realizations of the requirements of the essential grammar of a language-type. Of course there might also appear features which, while not universal, were very general; and such features might be scarcely less interesting, sometimes perhaps more interesting, than some features which were universal.

The question arises whether it might be possible to explain universality, or high generality, of features at either level. I think it might; that explanation might be of different kinds; and that some explanation might be broadly philosophical. For example, features at the first level might be correlated with categories which on general philosophical or metaphysical grounds could be argued to be fundamental in human thinking. And at the second level it might be shown that some ways of meeting the requirements of essential grammar were very much more natural than others.

My procedure will be as follows. First I shall produce some simple *a priori* sketches of the kind I have described—or rather some sketches of such sketches, for I shall not in every case go formally through each of the four stages in the design of a perspicuous grammar. Then I take two large generalizing steps each designed to represent one of the previously distinguished grammatical functions as a special though fundamental case of a more general function. Various incidental questions come up and are discussed *en route*. One principle I observe throughout is that of confining attention to sentences of a propositional or declarative kind. That is to say, if S (for sentence) is the fundamental grammatical category, then the general semantic form of S, for all our constructions, can be expressed in English by 'This is how things are'. It will be seen that I echo Wittgenstein's remark about the general propositional form. I hope this is a clear way to put it.

2. Language-Types 1 and 2

We begin with a language-type of almost idiotic simplicity. (In general, the early stages of this illustrative development will be somewhat tedious and jejune.) Any language of this type contains just two classes of semantically significant elements (for short, words) and allows of just one mode of combination of elements. Words of one class are correlated with individual substantial particulars, words of the other class with general characters or kinds of such particulars. We might call them particular names and general names or, better, *i*-words and *g*-words. The one mode of combination consists in linking an *i*-word and a *g*-word to produce a sentence. I describe the semantic outcome of such a combination in terms which echo the discussions of Part One: the resulting sentence presents a specified particular and a specified general character of particulars as belonging to, or assigned to, each other; i.e. what the sentence says is true if the particular exemplifies the character (the character characterizes the particular), false if not. This description is intended to be neutral as between various illocutionary modes in which the proposition might be propounded: e.g. by way of *instancing* the particular as an instance of the general character or of *describing* it as characterized by the general character. Within the combination the i-word has the function of specifying the assigned particular, the g-word has the function of specifying the assigned general character, and the combination as a whole yields a truth-valued specification of a state of affairs or possible fact of a certain kind, viz. the kind just described.

Evidently the essential grammar of such a language-type is very simply stated. It is simply the requirement that there should be some linkage-device to indicate when an i-word and a g-word are to be taken together as combined in the specified way to form a sentence. Unordered juxtaposition with sentence-interval would do. An ordering rule could be introduced but would be redundant unless it replaced the rule about sentence-interval. A name for the one mode of combination (e.g. 'predication'), names for syntactic classes (e.g. 'subject-phrase', 'predicate-phrase') and definitions of syntactic relations (e.g. 'subject of S', 'predicate of S') could be introduced as well. But they too would be redundant. Given the specification of the language-type, our two semantic classes (i-words and g-words) are also all the syntactic classes we need.

There is one question of some interest, however, which can be raised even in respect of this very simple language-type; can be raised and then put on one side. Suppose our i-words fall into two sub-classes, personal names (i_p-words) and non-animate material thing names (i_m-words). And suppose our g-words also fall into two sub-classes, say g_m-words and g_p-words, which are such that if we link a g_p-word to an i_m-word we find the result has that kind of semantically disturbing quality which has never been fully clarified but which we indicate with the phrase 'category-absurdity'; whereas any other combination (i.e. of g_p-word with i_p-word or of g_m-word with i_p- or i_m-word) is free from this disturbing quality. It has been suggested that an adequate grammar of a language should include rules, in the form of selection restrictions, forbidding such disturbing linkages. On the other hand it has been felt that it misrepresents the character of these sentences to call them ungrammatical.

Now it is clear, in terms of the present approach, that such sentences violate no rule of variable grammar. For the rules of variable grammar simply lay down how the requirements of essential grammar are to be fulfilled; and these requirements are simply that certain combinatory functions and certain relationships of sentence-parts entering into the combinations in question must, somehow or other, be clearly indicated and distinguished. If, then, the sentences are to be excluded at all, their exclusion must be effectively guaranteed at the very first stage of all, i.e. at the stage of specifying the language-type. But it would seem undesirable to try so to specify a language-type as to exclude in advance whatever, if admitted, would partake of the nature of self-contradiction or metaphor; and it is just the character of the semantically bizarre sentences we are considering that they partake of the nature of both. Evidently the theoretical framework in which I am working allows little scope for regarding category-absurdity as a species of ungrammaticalness; and I count this as a merit of the framework. This is not to say that our approach will cast no light on the nature of category-absurdity; and I think indeed it does cast some light on this.

Now let us contemplate a small enrichment of our language-type. We move from LT 1 to LT 2. All sentences of an LT 2 language, like all sentences of an LT 1 language, are apt for presenting a specified individual particular and a specified general character of particulars as assigned to each other. But LT 2 languages are richer than LT 1 languages in that they permit of other ways, besides the use of an i-word, for specifying the assigned particular in such a sentence. They include, besides i-words and g-words, another type of semantic element. This is the class of deictic or indexical distinguishers or t-words. This class has several sub-classes. These are (1) interlocutor distinguishers, two in number, the addresser- and the addressee-distinguishers, corresponding to English first and second person singular pronouns; (2) two vicinal distinguishers, comparable with English 'this' and 'that'; and (3) an expression for what I shall call bare contextual deixis, which would correspond roughly in one role to the singular definite article and in another to a third-person singular pronoun in one of *its* roles (cf. French 'le' and 'la'). Any of these deictic distinguishers can perform the functions allotted in LT 1 languages to i-words alone, i.e. the function of specifying, or identifyingly referring to, the assigned particular. But this function can also be performed, in LT 2 sentences, in another way. It can be performed by a deictic distinguisher of one of the last two sub-classes in linkage with one or more g-words. That is to say, in the essential grammar of LT 2 we have to recognize not only the *major linkage* of a particular-specifying sentence-part with a sentence-part having the function of complementary general character specification; we have also to recognize a *minor linkage* of *t*-words and *g*-words to produce a sentence-part with the function of particular-specification. We have a new type of combination taking its place inside the old type.

This creates a new requirement of essential grammar: the requirement, namely, that a *g*-element in a minor linkage should be distinguished as such from a *g*-element functioning as a major sentence-part in major linkage with such a combination.

How could this requirement be met? One way would be to introduce something like inflection for *g*-words: any *g*-word is to have one form when it functions as an element in a minor linkage, another when it functions as a major sentence-part with the role of complementary general character specification. Another way would be to exploit word- or phrase-order. For example, we could adopt the rule that all elements in a minor linkage must *precede* the *g*-word which has the major-part role of complementary general character specification; or the rule that the *g*-word with the latter role may come either at the end or the beginning of the sentence but that in either case the *t*-word which enters into the minor linkage must precede the other elements of that linkage. Or again we could adopt a more general phrase-order rule, in terms of major-part functions, from which a disambiguating rule of the type required would follow.

To develop this last possibility. Suppose we introduce functional definitions of the notions of subject and predicate for our language-type as follows. The subject is the sentence-part which has the function of specifying the assigned particular, the predicate the sentence-part which has the function of complementary general character specification. We can then define subject-phrase and predicate-phrase in abstraction from particular sentences as follows: a subject-phrase is an expression or combination of expressions which can serve as a subject; a predicate-phrase any expression which can serve as a predicate. The membership of these classes follows from the specification of the language-type. Thus all and only *g*-words are predicate phrases. Subject-phrases include all *i*-words, all *t*-words and also any set of expressions containing a *t*-word from either sub-class (2) or sub-class (3) together with one or more *g*-words. A simple general rule giving us as much variable grammar as we need would then be: any sentence of the language consists of a subject-phrase followed by a predicate-phrase. Of course this is a more restrictive rule than we actually need to satisfy the requirements of essential grammar. We gain simplicity at the cost of an excess of power. But this is perhaps characteristic of actual grammars.

It will be noted that in languages of LT 2, items of some semantic types are allotted a plurality of functional roles or semantico-syntactic functions. Thus t-words of sub-classes (2) and (3) can function both as subjects and as subject-constituents, and g-words can function both as subject-constituents and as predicates. These words, that is to say, can function as major sentence-parts entering directly into major linkages, or as elements in minor linkages, the outcomes of which enter into major linkages. With the given rule, however, no formal differentiation would be necessary to mark this variation of function.

3. Language-Type 3: relations

So far our g-expressions have all been conceived, to use the language of logic, as one-place predicates. Let our next step in enrichment—the step from LT 2 to LT 3—be the introduction of a class of general words correlated with dyadic relational characters of particulars; the introduction, that is, of two-place predicates. We will call them 'g_2-words' and our previous class of g-words 'g_1-words'. Our g_2-words divide into semantico-logical sub-classes in ways important for grammar. The most obviously important division is into the logically familiar classes of the symmetrical and the non-symmetrical. (I use this distinction strictly dichotomously, i.e. the non-symmetrical class includes the asymmetrical.)

Let us suppose, first, that we had to deal only with the first of these two types—with expressions specifying symmetrical relations. What amendments would we have to make to our grammar? Note first that we have not fully specified LT 3 in saying that languages of this type contain, over and above the semantic types that LT 2 languages contain, words of a new semantic type, viz. g_2-words. We must also say into what type of combination these new elements can enter to yield what semantic outcome. And the predictable answer to this is that just as g_1-words can enter into major linkage with a single sentence-part, having the particular-specifying function, to yield a sentence in which (as we can indifferently say) the particular is presented as characterized by the character or the character as characterizing the particular, so g_2-words can enter into major linkage with both of two sentence-parts, each having the particular-specifying function, to yield a sentence in which two specified particulars are presented as related to each other by a specified relation *or* a specified relation is presented as relating two particulars *or* one of two particulars is presented as related by a specified relation to another *or* the other as so related to the one. The point of this tedious listing of alternative descriptions is to caution us against any premature grouping of sentence-parts. The moral of essential grammar we can draw is this: that any grammar of an LT 3 language must provide somehow for a major linkage of *three* parts, two particular-specifying and one relation-specifying, in addition to what is already provided for in less rich grammars, viz. a two-part major linkage of one particular-specifying and one character-specifying sentence part.

This requirement of the essential grammar for LT 3 brings with it another requirement. The possibility of specifying particulars by means of combinations of elements entering into minor linkage with each other means that any variable grammar of an LT 3 language must provide some indication of which elements are to be taken with which as forming such a compound: it must provide some means of ensuring against ambiguity as regards the composition of minor, particular-specifying linkages. This result would not be secured, for example, by simply extending and adapting to our new sentences the rule just contemplated for our old sentences: i.e. the rule that all elements which contribute to particular-specification must precede the element with the function of complementary specification of general character (including, now, general relational character). For even if we add, say, a 'neighbouring' rule, that no element of a minor linkage is separated from another element of that linkage by anything which is not an element, there would still be room for several different readings of such sentence-patterns as

$$t\alpha\phi\gamma t\beta g_2$$

where the Greek letters represent g_1-words. There would, for example, be three possible ways of dividing a sentence of this pattern to yield two minor linkages: the division could fall between α and ϕ, between ϕ and γ or between γ and t. Division into particular-specifying parts in general could even fall between the first t and α. Obviously there are several possible ways of dealing with this possibility of ambiguity. I list four:

(1) We could require that the relation-specifying expression was always interposed between the two particular-specifying expressions. We might call this a *major positioning device*.

(2) We could introduce a distinctive *inflection* for all the elements of

one (it would not matter which) of the two particular-specifying combinations.

(3) We could exploit the possibility of ordering the elements entering into a minor linkage: e.g. for the language-types so far specified it would be sufficient, in conjunction with the neighbouring rule, to introduce the rule, already considered in relation to LT 2, that the *t*-word should precede all other elements in a minor linkage. This could be called a *minor positioning device*.

(4) We could introduce an extraneous marker of some kind, all the elements of one particular-specifying expression to be on one side of the marker, all the elements of the other to be on the other side. In spoken discourse this would not have to be a syllable or something composed of syllables. It could be a matter of pause or intonation. But suppose it rather to be some spoken or written element, inserted between the two compounds. Then it would be an interestingly new kind of expression, something of which we could clearly say that it had a purely syntactic or grammatical significance, that it was semantically empty (even though it contributes to overall semantic interpretation). We might call this the device of the *separate syntactic marker*. There is a resemblance here with the second suggestion, regarding inflection: in that if the inflection, say, consisted in the addition of a standard termination, we could say exactly the same thing of that termination as we say of the separate syntactic marker, viz. that it had a purely syntactic significance or that it had no semantic content of its own though it contributed to overall semantic interpretation.

Let us give a name to the function which we might choose one or another of these various devices to perform for a variable grammar of a LT 3 language. Let us call it the function of *term-separating*. Once we drop the assumption that all the g_2-words of LT 3 languages specify symmetrical relations, it is clear that while the function of term-separating is necessary to the unambiguous interpretation of sentences of such languages, it is not sufficient. It is clear that something more is needed. The only new functions we have so far mentioned in connection with LT 3 are: (i) that of providing for three-part major linkages as well as two-part major linkages; (ii) that of distinguishing two minor linkages from each other in the sense of indicating which elements belong to which. But with non-symmetrical relations admitted, we must be able to distinguish particular-specifying expressions from each other in a further sense. What is in question is the distinction we normally signalize in English by the difference in position of the two singular terms in such sentences as 'The old man loves the young woman' or 'The old man is heavier than the young woman'. It is what accounts for the difference in meaning between these sentences and the sentences 'The young woman loves the old man' or 'The young woman is heavier than the old man'. As we called the first kind of distinguishing *term-separating*, so we might call this second kind *term-ordering*.

It is easy to illustrate and name this function, and clear that it is necessary. What is not quite so clear, I think, is what this function is. Perhaps it is something we think we understand because it is so familiar. We talk happily about the *direction* (or *sense*)[1] of a non-symmetrical relation; and we can give formal definitions of the notion of an ordered pair. It does not follow that we really have a clear grasp of the semantic (or semantico-syntactic) feature or features that are in question, and it seems to me possible that we do not clearly distinguish a familiar mode of representation of those features from what is represented. This, at least, is my excuse for what follows—which, if there is no problem such as I seem to feel, will seem at best a merely decorative digression; and which, if there is, *may* seem too close to the problem to count as a solution.

Logicians customarily divide non-symmetrical two-place predicates into those which are asymmetrical and those which are not. This is a sharp division. I want to begin by proposing a tentative semantic division which, for actual languages, is not a sharp one, though we may suppose it to be so for languages of LT 3. It is a division between what I shall call *essentially directed relations* and others. There are two types of clear cases of essentially directed relations. One type of clear case is any in which the minimal requirement for the relation to hold between two actual objects is that one of the two should perform some action or hold some attitude or be in some state of mind which is 'directed at' the other or has the other as its 'intentional' object. I call this the minimal requirement because it is not necessarily excluded that the relation is reciprocal. Examples would be the relations signified by English 'seek', 'love', 'avoid', 'admire', 'detest'. Another clear type of case is any in which one term of the relation is conceived of as affecting the other, as responsible for a change in state, or deviation or interruption of course, of the other: e.g. 'hit', 'obstruct', 'liberate', 'wound'. Again, mutuality is not necessarily excluded. The similarity between the two types of case which I mark by calling them 'essentially directed'

[1] In what follows, to avoid confusion, I shall not use 'sense' in this special, but only in its more general, sense.

relations could be marked also by saying that in each type of case, when any of these relations is thought of as holding between actualities, something is conceived of as causal or intentional *object*, and something as causal or intentional *origin*, of the relation. And this is so even when, as is sometimes the case, only one thing is involved, as both object and origin, and even when, of two things involved, each has both positions *vis-à-vis* the other.

The two types of case of essentially directed relation are not mutually exclusive. They may overlap, as in some cases of intentional action, e.g. 'murder'. Equally clearly, they may sometimes be quite distinct. An intentional object of an attitude or action may be quite unaffected thereby; and one thing may be affected in a certain way by another without being the intentional object of any attitude of the other, which may, indeed, be incapable of intentional attitudes. Again, the two types of case may exhibit a certain complementarity. If x impresses y, y is the affected object; if y admires x, x is the intentional object. But even if 'x impresses y' and 'y admires x' always and necessarily go together, they are not each other's true semantic converses. One represents things under the aspect of an *effect* which x has on y; the other under the aspect of an *attitude* which y has towards x. For true semantic converses, we turn rather, in English, to the passive forms of each: for 'x impresses y' to 'y is impressed by x', for 'y admires x' to 'x is admired by y'. These passive transformations leave the roles of the terms unchanged. If we say that John impresses Mary, we represent John as origin and Mary as object of the relation; and so we do if we say that Mary is impressed by John.

Suppose we adopted the assumption that all those g_2-words of a language of LT 3 which signified non-symmetrical relations signified essentially directed relations. Then the nature of the function we are trying to clarify could, it might seem, be readily explained for such a language. If, in such a language, we frame a sentence presenting two particulars as related by a non-symmetrical relation, we must indicate which term is being presented as the origin and which as the object of that relation. To do this will *be* to perform the function I named 'term-ordering'. For the performance of this new function it may not be be necessary to introduce new formal devices; for we simply may be able to put existing arrangements to further uses. And in fact it is easy to see that there is no term-separating device among those I listed which does not automatically put at our disposal a term-ordering device. Methods (1), (3) and (4) of term-separating all presuppose that one term wholly precedes the other in the sentence. So long as we are dealing with symmetrical relations only—where all we need to ensure is term-separation—it makes no difference to overall interpretation which term comes first and which comes second. We can treat phrase-order as indifferent so long as we have clear phrase-separation. But phrase-order is now at our disposal as something which we need not treat as indifferent, but can use to indicate term-ordering. Method (2), the inflectional method, unless it is combined with the neighbouring rule, does not automatically put phrase-order at our disposal. But the situation is essentially the same. So long as separation only is in question it does not matter which term-phrase receives the separating inflection, so long as one does. But when term-ordering comes into question, we can *make* it matter; we can make it the decisive factor in term-ordering.

Suppose that the term-separating device adopted in our variable grammar is one which does put phrase-order at our disposal. Then it might seem that we could simply adopt, as our required device of variable grammar, the term-ordering rule that, say, the phrase specifying the term of origin is to precede the phrase specifying the object-term of the relation. But this suggestion is open to the obvious objection that unless we are to prejudice the possibility of the existence of a form corresponding to the English passive, we must restrict the application of the rule as we have it to a form corresponding to the English active form, and be prepared to add the converse rule for the converse form; but this would imply an independent grasp of the distinction between the two forms, and of such a distinction we have before us no independent account.

A reply to this objection might be attempted on the following lines. The rule proposed, it might be said, is a rule of 'basic' variable grammar, and by no means excludes the possibility of transformations which would reverse phrase-order without change of semantic content. Indeed, by looking at the matter in this way, we can better understand the name and nature of the 'passive' form as we have it, seeing it as something essentially secondary and derivative. Its name registers the fact that the phrase designating the object-term of the essentially directed relation occupies the place held in the primary form by the term of origin.

Whatever the local merits of this reply, it suffers finally from the deep deficiency which infects the whole account; viz. lack of generality. It must surely be possible to give a single, comprehensive account of the term-ordering function, an account which applies to all sentences containing g_2-words for non-symmetrical relations. It would be highly counter-intuitive to suppose otherwise. Our initial restriction of g_2-words to words for essentially directed relations was quite unrealistic; yet the distinction between terms of causal or intentional origin and causal or intentional object-terms has application only to essentially directed relations. Hence any account of the term-ordering function which incorporates an essential reference to that distinction must be finally unacceptable.

So we turn our attention to dyadic non-symmetrical relations which either clearly do not fall, or do not clearly fall, into the category of the essentially directed. Many such relations order their terms in respect of what might, in a narrower or a broader sense, be called 'relative position'. Relative position may be, quite straightforwardly, relative spatial position: 'to the left of', 'to the right of', 'above', 'below'. It may be position on any degree-scale, e.g. of youth or beauty; and all comparatives fall under this general characterization: 'older/younger than', 'more/less beautiful than', 'richer/poorer than', 'hotter/colder than' and so on. Again, it may be a matter of relative position in some specific legal or social nexus: as 'ward of', 'guardian of': 'debtor of', 'creditor of'. One might be inclined to speak of relations of this again not very sharply defined class as 'ordering relations', were the phrase not already appropriated by logicians for another classification.

The contrast between such relations as these and essentially directed relations emerges clearly if we consider relations of each class together with their converses. If we replace 'John admires Mary' by 'Mary is admired by John', 'John hit Mary' by 'Mary was hit by John', John is still represented as the origin, Mary as the object of the attitude or action. But if we replace 'John is to the left of Mary' with 'Mary is to the right of John' or 'John is older than Mary' with 'Mary is younger than John', there is no comparable general point to be made. There is a kind of parity of converses in the second class of cases; there is no one converse-invariant general way of regarding any two-termed fact which such a pair of sentences might be apt for stating. The same contrast is observable in the case of other relations which are not essentially directed but which we might hesitate to describe as ordering their terms in respect of relative position: e.g. 'husband of' and 'wife of' in a society where legal equality of the sexes prevails.

So, in the case of all non-symmetrical relations which are not essentially directed relations, we lose the converse-invariant distinction of object and origin. But from the point of view of achieving a general characterization of the term-ordering function, the loss is no loss at all or is the loss only of an encumbrance. For it helps us to realize that it is essential to the sense of any non-symmetrical dyadic relation-expression whatever that it selects or picks out or applies to *one* of the terms it relates in a way in which it does not select or pick out or apply to the other; and the general character of the difference in sense between any such expression and its converse is reflected in the fact that if both were to be used in turn to report correctly the same two-itemed fact, then each must select in this special way the item the other does *not* select. To put the point metaphorically: we can pivot our report of such a two-itemed fact on either of its terms; if we pivot it on one term, then we use one of a pair of converse relation-expressions for our report, if we pivot it on the other term, then we use the other member of the pair of expressions. Or, to change the image: we can look at the same two-itemed fact from the standpoint of either of its terms; if we look at it from the standpoint of one, we get one non-symmetrical relation, if we look at it from the standpoint of the other, we get the converse relation.

But we can dispense with metaphor. We can make the point emerge in its full literal force by reflecting on alternative notations for performing the function of term-ordering. In English we write 'John is older than Mary' or 'Mary is younger than John'. Instead we might write:

> Of the (unordered) pair, John and Mary, related by the age-difference relation, Mary is (the) younger

or

> Of the (unordered) pair, John and Mary, related by the age-difference relation, John is (the) older.

The preamble is identical in both cases and mentions both related items, presenting them as related by the symmetrical relation of age-difference; but selection of one of the pair of converses carries with it the selection, for a *second* mention, of *one only* of the pair of terms.

Let us call the selected term the *primary* term of a non-symmetrical relation and the other term the *secondary* term. We might represent the general form of propositions of this kind as follows:

$$\text{Of the pair, } a \text{ and } b, \text{ related by the R–}\check{\text{R}}\text{ relation} \begin{cases} (1) \text{ R} \ldots \\ (2) \check{\text{R}} \ldots \end{cases}$$

To complete such a proposition we select just *one* of the numbered expressions following the bracket and fill its empty place with just *one* of the two terms. This is the primary term.

There are many variant ways of making essentially the same point. To give one more example: we can imagine a notation in which

(1) $\left.\begin{matrix} a \\ b \end{matrix}\right\}$ to the immediate left of   (3) $\left.\begin{matrix} a \\ b \end{matrix}\right\}$ younger

(2) $\left.\begin{matrix} a \\ b \end{matrix}\right\}$ to the immediate right of   (4) $\left.\begin{matrix} a \\ b \end{matrix}\right\}$ older

are all *complete* propositions of which (1) is equivalent to (2) and (3) to (4)—the relative positions of the names having no significance at all. But though complete propositions, they are more general, less specific, than propositions we can obtain from them by ringing *one* of the terms in each case. In this notation, term-ringing is our term-selecting device. *Mutatis mutandis*, it works like gap-filling in the other notation: so that

$\left.\begin{matrix} ⓐ \\ b \end{matrix}\right\}$ younger   is equivalent to $\left.\begin{matrix} a \\ ⓑ \end{matrix}\right\}$ older

and is incompatible with $\left.\begin{matrix} a \\ ⓑ \end{matrix}\right\}$ younger.

Now we can give a *general* characterization of the term-ordering function. It is the function of indicating which is the primary and which is the secondary term of a non-symmetrical relation. The characterization is quite general and applies as well to essentially directed as to non-essentially-directed relations. What I spoke of as the 'term of origin' of an essentially directed relation will figure as primary term in a sentence containing the 'active' form of a verb for that relation and as secondary term in an equivalent sentence containing the 'passive' form; and *vice versa* for the 'object-term'. The distinction we began with, between essentially directed relations and others, was of no help in solving our general problem, though, as just now suggested, it may have relevance to other questions about the grammar of our relation-expressions and their converses; but I shall not pursue these questions here.

I have taken this long and possibly rather tedious way round the question of term-ordering because, as I suggested, it is perhaps particularly difficult for us to separate in thought what has to be indicated from the standard way of indicating it. When we try to say what we are representing, we are prone simply to stammer out some variation on a standard mode of representation. And the phrase 'direction of a relation' offers no illumination of itself; for it either simply repeats the image of a mode of representation or diverts us with other images appropriate only to a limited range of cases.

The treatment, of course, has been abstract and, from the point of view of the study of actual languages, grossly over-simplified. There is, for example, no reason to suppose that in actual languages we shall find just one uniform means of indicating term-ordering. We may find a great variety of means, more or less closely reflecting semantic type-differences. To mention only inflection, we can find in Latin accusative, dative, genitive and ablative inflection all serving this purpose in different types of case. Again, there is every reason to expect to find structure *within* some of the types of relational expression I have spoken of, e.g. comparatives.

Now to complete the task of choosing a variable grammar for a language of LT 3. Let us suppose that for term-separating we choose some device which ensures that one sentence-part with the particular-specifying function wholly precedes the other. Suppose, in particular, we adopt the major positioning device, i.e. the interposition of the g_2-word between the two particular-specifying parts. And let us suppose that our solution to the term-ordering requirement is to rule that in the case of a non-symmetrical relation the primary term comes first and the secondary term second.

Stage 3 in the design of a perspicuous grammar for a language of LT 3 is now complete. All the requirements of essential grammar for LT 3 have now been met by a choice among possible devices. But what of Stage 4? What of the systematic presentation of the grammar?

Let us recall the presentation of the chosen variable grammar of a language of LT 2. Functional definitions of *subject* and *predicate*, based on the specification of the language-type, were first supplied, then further definitions, based on these, of *subject-phrase* and *predicate-phrase*. The general character of the membership of these syntactic classes followed from these definitions together with the specification of the language-type. The chosen variable grammar for the LT 2 language was then encapsulated in a very simple rule, which ran: every sentence of the language consists of a subject-phrase followed by a predicate-phrase.

It is clear that either this rule or these definitions or both would have to be revised if we were to use the same terminology in systematically presenting our chosen variable grammar for a language of LT 3. The revision could be effected in a variety of ways. But I am going to pass them over and leave the question of systematic presentation on one side. That a systematic presentation is possible is clear; for we have already informally presented a complete and perspicuous variable grammar for a language of LT 3. But my main reason for passing over the question is that I want to stretch and extend the functional notions which underlie the original definitions of subject and predicate in quite other ways, and in the meantime wish to keep the field as clear as possible of definitional complications.

4. Further minor enrichments : space–time indication

Obviously, as we enrich our language-types, the affair of going through each of the four stages—specification of language-type; deduction of essential grammar; consideration of possible variable grammars; systematic presentation of a particular variable grammar—would become more and more elaborate. I have already, as just remarked, let myself off the last stage. And now, on the assumption that the principle of the whole approach is clear, I am going to relax things still further and discuss further enrichments in a yet more informal style. I shall symbolize this relaxation by dropping the device of numbered language-types. I shall still be talking of specified language-types and their essential grammars; but I shall not pause at every stage to inquire how the essential requirements might be met, still less to set out formally the rules for a variable grammar capable of meeting them. With these economies I hope the sooner to reach, or to come within sight of, the goal: some grasp of the relation between the logic-based conception of subject and predicate treated of in Part One and a more comprehensive conception to be developed in the succeeding chapters.

But before undertaking any radical broadening of our language-types, I want to introduce two relatively unproblematic kinds of enrichment.

All sentences of our language-types so far specify states of affairs involving substances (or continuant spatio–temporal particulars). They do so by specifying particular substances and general characters or relations and combining the specifying expressions propositionally. Now some characters or relations are permanencies or relative permanencies: standing characters or relations of individuals or couples that exemplify them. The individuals or couples concerned exemplify them, to speak roughly, all the time and wherever they are. So it is, for example, with the relation of *being brothers*. But many, perhaps most, characters and relations are not like this. The question, '*Where* and *when* does the state of affairs of Tom and William *being brothers* obtain?' is not a question that arises. But the question, '*Where* and *when* does the state of affairs of Tom and William *fighting* (*each other*) obtain?' is a question that may arise. So far our language-types are not supplied with the means of answering (or of asking) such questions. We continue to eschew all but declarative sentences. But we may now recognize, alongside the functions of particular-specification and general character specification, the function of *situational space–time indication*.

There is a certain asymmetry here which is worth remarking on parenthetically. This asymmetry is really a matter of what it means to give an individually distinguishing specification of a particular *situation* of a certain general type. If we specify the particular individual(s) involved and, *with sufficient definiteness*, a particular time, it follows that we have uniquely specified the particular situation. But the same consequence does not follow if we specify the particular individual(s) involved and a particular place. For the same general type of situation involving the same particular individuals could have different, temporally separated instances at the same place. But it could not have different, spatially separated instances at the same time. For this is inconsistent with the supposition that the same particular individuals are involved. Hence time-indication has, in principle, a role in the unique specification of a situation involving particular individuals which place-indication has not.

Since every utterance has a space–time origin, the device of deixis is available to give space–time indications of the incidence of a situation. And we know the device is used. We have in English deictic adverbs of place—'here', 'there', 'nearby', 'far away'—and of time—'yesterday', 'tomorrow', 'soon', 'long ago', 'now'. And we have, in many languages, verbal auxiliaries and verbal inflections to indicate tense. The categories of verb and abverb are not categories we have introduced. But this does not prevent us from trying to understand why this association of situational space–time deixis with the verb is so widely prevalent. We can, that is to say, ask a related question about the word- and phrase-classes we have recognized in our limited languages. We can ask: if situational space–time deixis is to be associated with one part of the sentence rather than another, with which part might it most naturally be associated? Let us concentrate, to begin with, on time.

The question is not particularly easy to answer. But here are some hints. Suppose we were dealing in an ontology—actually an impossible or at least highly dubious one—in which the basic individuals were not particular continuants but what philosophers (toying with the notion from the inescapable viewpoint of their own ontology) are prone to call time-slices of particular continuants. Then it would seem that *individual* identification would tend to carry with it all that we need for situational time-indication; and, to that extent, independent *situational* time-indication would become superfluous. No conclusion follows strictly from this about the association of situational time-indication with one sentence-part rather than another, given an ontology of continuant particulars. But it at least tends to suggest that association of situational time-indication with particular-specification is *alien* to our ontology.

Here is another more definite point. We do in our *developed* language of continuant particulars have a clear use for expressions like 'the former President', 'the future King' and so on; where a time-indicating word modifies a *g*-word by way of contributing to particular-specification. But of course the time-indicating words here are precisely not performing the function of situation-time-indicating. The latter function is one that must clearly be kept distinct from the former. We must run no risk of confusion between them.

This is perhaps sufficient to indicate that there is a case against associating situational time-indication with the particular-specifying part of the sentence and, hence, if any such association is to be made, a case for making it with the phrase specifying general character or relation. For there are no parallel or corresponding objections to making the association in this way.

So far as we have gone in the specification of our language-types, however, we have as yet no reason for insisting on any particular association here. We could simply regard explicit situational time-indication as a further function which may be performed in addition to the major functions already recognized, and the sentence-part performing that function as a sentence-part to be simply *added* in major linkage with other major sentence-parts. Beyond the general requirement of linkage of parts into a sentence, no further syntactical requirement can yet be insisted on. We could, for example, imagine expressions with the force of *Past, Present, Future,* just added to our sentences anywhere, provided they did not violate some neighbouring rule for the parts of a minor linkage or disrupt any comparable existing requirements of syntactical arrangement.[2] Let us, then, suppose some such elements added to our language-types.

[2] Compare the freedom of positioning which some temporal adverbs and adverbial phrases enjoy in some simple English sentences: e.g. the number of possible positions for the phrase 'at that time' in a sentence otherwise composed of the words 'England was at war with France'.

Now to consider deictic space- or place-indicators. It is easier to see our way here. We have already allowed for deictic distinguishers with some spatial force as parts or wholes of subject-phrases (phrases specifying particulars). Now we are to consider the possibility of deictic indicators with spatial force for locating situations; and the case against associating such indicators with phrases specifying particulars is clear at once. There would be an obvious risk of ambiguity. Various languages contain significant suggestions here: Latin has 'hic' for 'here' and for 'this', French has 'ici' and 'là' and also 'ceci', 'cela', 'ce-*x*-ci', 'ce-*x*-là'. In any form of communication *pointing* can be used *either* to pick out, or to help to pick out, a particular substance *or* to indicate where some situation is, was or will be realized. Suppose, in the extended sense of 'same expression' which I have already introduced, we had the same expression corresponding roughly to both 'this' and 'here' and the same expression corresponding roughly to both 'that' and 'there'; i.e. that any language of our currently considered language-type contains a single semantic item for what we will call 'nearer vicinal deixis' and a single semantic item for what we will call 'farther vicinal deixis', where each of these single items may serve either to help with particular-specification or to help with situation-location. Then we will need formal differentiation of function, either by means of positioning or by means of variation in the form of the expression or both. For we shall certainly need to know when the item is to be taken as entering into particular-specification and when it is not. In the first case, the spatially deictic expression must obviously be taken with other elements of a particular-specifying linkage as forming part of that linkage. In the second, if the spatially deictic expression is to be associated with some one or other part of the sentence, then it must be associated with the part which specifies the general character or relation to which the particular or particulars are presented as assigned. But again, for the moment, there seems to be no compelling reason against representing situational space-indication, like situational time-indication, as a function to be discharged by a major sentence-part entering into major linkage with other such parts.

One more minor enrichment is to be introduced before the first radical broadening of our language-types. This enrichment consists in providing for the combination of particular-specification with deictic space–time indication alone. That is, we provide for sentences in which a particular-specifying expression stands directly in major linkage with a sentence-part with the function of space–time indication, but in which there is no *major* part with the function of specifying a general character or relation. These will be sentences roughly comparable with ordinary English 'John is here now', 'The old man was there previously' and so on. It is quite a departure in that for the first time it will not be the case that one of the parts of a major linkage has the function of specifying a general character or relation to be assigned to a particular or particulars.

4
Substantiation
and its
Modes

1. Special case and general function

Now for a rather radical broadening of our language-types. All of the sentence-types we have so far considered have this in common: that each specifies a type of substance-involving situation or state of affairs and is apt for the expression of a proposition to the effect that such a situation or state of affairs obtains. Within this general sentential role we can distinguish complementary functions of major sentence-parts; and, correspondingly, within sentences of our types we can distinguish the major sentence-parts to which these functions are assigned. Thus we distinguish (1) the function of identifying specification of individual substantial particulars from (2) that of complementary general character-or-relation specification and we distinguish both of these from (3) the functions of space- and/or time-indication. We have allowed not just for one but for a variety, though a limited variety, of ways of combining these functions; and hence for a limited variety of major linkages of major sentence-parts. Thus—our latest enrichment—we can have major linkage of sentence-parts having functions (1) and (3) without a further part having function (2). We can have (1) linked with (2) with

99

or without explicit (3). We can have two doses of (1), linked with (2) or with both (2) and (3), under the condition that the general character specified under (2) is relational.

The proposal I want now to consider, though it involves a radical broadening of our language-types, yet involves no change in the characterization just given of general sentence-function, viz., that each sentence specifies a type of substance-involving situation or state of affairs or possible fact and is apt for the expression of a proposition to the effect that such a situation or state of affairs or possible fact obtains. Nor does it involve any major addition to the recognized modes of combination. It consists simply in recognizing function (1), the function I have called particular-specification, as a special case of a more general function which I shall call *substantiation* and which includes as a special case—a very special case—individually identifying (or *i.i.*)[1] *substantiation*; and hence includes (1).

It is generally characteristic of sentences of languages of our so far admitted language-types that the particular-specifying phrases they contain, when their reference in use is grasped, serve to identify the items they are applied to *as* the particular instances they are *of* some general kind or sort for which the language contains a g_1-word. This is obviously true in all cases in which the particular-specifying phrase actually contains a sortal g_1-word; and I shall take it that it is true for all *i*-words as well. As we saw in discussing a proposal derived from Geach,[2] we cannot be sure that this correlation of *i*-word with g_1-kind-word is of uniform maximum specificity for all speakers and hearers. This does not matter; such uniformity of correlation as this is not required for my purposes. It is sufficient, and more than sufficient, to assume some standing correlation, of relatively low specificity. Thus we take it that to every phrase of either class in use is correlated, in the understanding of speaker and hearer, some sortal g_1-word: as perhaps, to phrases comparable with English 'John' or 'that man' a sortal corresponding to 'man'; to phrases comparable to English 'Mary' or 'that woman' a sortal corresponding to 'woman'; to phrases corresponding to English 'Tom' or 'that cat' a sortal corresponding to 'cat'.

Now consider two sentences of our so far admitted language-types, of which the first, S1, corresponds to English 'John pursues Mary' and of which the second, S2, corresponds to English 'Tom is drowning'.

---

[1] I use this abbreviation sometimes for 'individually identifying', sometimes for 'individual identification'.

[2] See above, Part One, Chapter 2, Section 4.

Then suppose our language-types somehow or other enriched to allow of sentences of a quite new type not so far provided for. We can illustrate the semantic character of our new type of sentence as follows. Think of a certain general type of substance-involving situation: e.g. that of a man pursuing a woman; or that of a cat drowning. Then a typical sentence of our new kind might be a sentence apt for expressing a proposition to the effect that a situation of such a general type obtained, *without* specifying a particular man or a particular woman or a particular cat. Suppose some language of our enriched language-type includes two such sentences, one for each of these two types of situation. Call these sentences S3 and S4.

Now any speaker's or hearer's grasp of propositions expressed by sentences S1 and S2 will, by our previous provision, include, though it is not exhausted by, a grasp of something more general as specified in each proposition, viz. precisely what is to be expressed by sentences S3 and S4. In view of the special nature of this relation, we could say that all the functional needs created by the specification of the semantic character of our new sentences are already implicitly met, and more than met, by the functional capacity of our old sentences. There is no need to introduce any fundamentally new functional combination to make room for our new sentences; it will suffice to recognize particular-specification as a special, identifying case of a more general function. Just as, in our old sentences, particular-specifying sentence-parts may enter into major linkage with g_2-words or g_1-words in a sentence apt for expressing a proposition to the effect that a situation of a certain general type obtains, *a situation specified in respect of the identity of particular substances involved*, so, in our new sentences, appropriate sortals may enter by themselves into major linkage with g_2-words in a sentence apt for expressing a proposition to the effect that *some* situation of that general type obtains—*but this time without any individual identification of particular substances involved*. If, disregarding time-indication, we represent our old sentences, S1 and S2, by

S1   John + pursue + Mary   S2   Tom + drown

then, in a parallel way, we may represent our new sentences S3 and S4 by

S3   man + pursue + woman   S4   cat + drown.

The proposal, then, is to substitute 'substantiation' for 'particular-specification' in our functional descriptions and to regard the latter as a special case of the former. The proposal evidently invites elaboration. Are we to introduce a variety of modes of substantiation or to be content with two species, individually-identifying and non-individually-identifying; and, if the former, what new semantic resources shall we need? More fundamentally, the proposal might seem to invite scepticism. Can we really give a clear general account of this supposed function of substantiation as opposed to what must be represented as the distinct and complementary function of complementary general character specification? We can certainly distinguish between what is now claimed to be a special case of this supposed general function—the case called 'i.i. substantiation'—and complementary general character specification. This distinction we already have. But this distinction, as we have it, yields us no general account of the supposed general function of substantiation. If we set this 'special case' aside, and introduce no new semantic elements, then we have no materials available for substantiation except the general class of *g*-words, to which materials available for complementary general character specification also belong. So how are we to explain the supposed difference in function? Scepticism is reinforced if we turn to the grammar of current logical notation. It is easy enough to spot the sentences which, in a language with that grammar, would replace, or do duty for, the sentences of our new class. They are sentences beginning with existential quantifiers binding variables which figure in conjoined following clauses. But no difference in syntactical role is explicitly represented in the schemata of these sentences between general terms, all alike in predicative position. At most we can distinguish, syntactically, between general terms in respect of number of place-holders, i.e. between one-place, two-place, . . . n-place predicates.

Let us turn back to the general characterization of the semantic character of all sentences so far considered, whether of the old variety or of the new. Each such sentence, I said, specifies a type of substance-involving situation or state of affairs and is apt for the expression of a proposition to the effect that such a situation or state of affairs obtains. The question is whether we are obliged (or able) to recognize, in the case of every such sentence, a distinction between a substantiating part and a part which complements it by completing the specification of situation-type or state of affairs. But what, after all, should be the difficulty? Formerly, we had the sharp distinction between the function of specifying just *what*, or *which*, particular substance or substances were involved and the function or functions of completing the specification of the state of affairs involving them. Shall we not still have a distinction between the function of specifying what *sort* of substance, or *what-like* substance, is involved and that of completing the specification of the state of affairs concerned?

Rhetorical questions, doubtless, are not enough. So let us turn to differences in semantic type among g-words and show how these are related to this difference in function. We have, first, the general distinction between g_2-words, signifying types of relation which individual substances may stand in, or enter into, with other individual substances, and g_1-words signifying non-relational general characters. And as far as relational sentences of our new type are concerned, this suffices to enforce the difference of function. With i.i. gone, we still specify a general type of situation of a relational kind involving substances as the terms of the relation; and the contrast of roles between relational character specification and indication of types of substantial terms still holds good even though no substantial terms are now individually identified. All the requirements of essential grammar (term-separation and term-ordering) for the i.i. case are still requirements for the non-i.i. case, and we need have no qualms about clearing the general role-distinction of substantiation, on the one hand, and general-character-specification in major linkage with it, on the other, of any suspicion of fuzziness in this case. Nor is the presence of sortals in any way required in the substantiating parts: something white following something red (or something unspeakable pursuing something uneatable) provides just as clear a case for role-distinction, as the case of a man pursuing a woman.

The distinction between g_2-words and g_1-words is not the only relevant distinction of semantic type. There are relevant distinctions among g_1-words themselves. Let us assume in particular that in languages of all our language-types g_1-words fall clearly into one or another of the following three groups: (1) those which signify *kinds* or *sorts* of individual substances (i.e. sortals, which I shall now also call *nominals*: *general* nominals, as opposed to individual names or individual nominals); (2) those which signify qualities or attributes of individual substances (I shall call these *adjectivals*); and (3) those which signify types of changes which individual substances may enter into—be they actions or undergoings or other kinds of event or process (these I shall call *verbals*). These names—nominals, adjectivals, verbals—are not, of course, to be confused with the ordinary grammatical classifications of noun, adjective and verb, which incorporate reference to the formal arrangements of variable grammars. They are, rather, strictly *semantic* classifications, though the point now of making them is to associate them with differences of semantico-syntactic function.

The difference of function in question, of course, is that between substantiation and complementary general character specification. Intuitively one would think that, if and when the functional difference holds in the absence of g_2-words then, other things being equal, nominals are the most apt for the substantiating role, and nominals and adjectivals, separately or in combination, are more apt for the substantiating role than verbals, the latter more apt for the role of complementary general character-specification in relation to the former. This intuition is correct; and I shall soon produce supporting and, I hope, explanatory evidence for it. But, first, there are two important qualifications to be made. One is the general and cautionary point that other semantic differences, finer than this broad threefold classification allows for, may also be relevant to role-distinction. The other concerns the saving phrase 'other things being equal'. It is implicit in the terms of the introduction of the notion of substantiation that where i.i. appears on the scene, the i.i. linkage pre-empts the substantiating role, whatever the relative semantic ranking of g-words within and without it. But we must also be prepared to allow for, though we have not yet introduced, a variety of modes of non-i.i. substantiation—associated, say, with pluralization, quantification, enumeration—and these too may easily over-ride the intuitive, semantic ranking. We have really made things gratuitously difficult for ourselves by simply contemplating the elimination of i.i. without considering the possible variety of modes of non-i.i. substantiation. But confidence may be gained from surmounting a gratuitous difficulty.

2. Some supporting evidence

Now for the supporting evidence I spoke of. It takes the form of a little essay in explanation of a feature of the grammar (the 'surface grammar') of English. So it is, in a sense, a digression from the main theme; but may nevertheless cast some light on it.

In ordinary English there occur many sentences which might be described in the language of *Word and Object*[3]—and indeed are described in that book—in the following way: they consist of an indefinite singular term in referential position (or, as we might say, in subject position) coupled or combined with a general term in predicative position. For example: 'A boy is drowning', 'A girl has just telephoned'.

[3] W. V. O. Quine, *Word and Object*, Cambridge, Mass., M.I.T. Press, 1960.

The language of *Word and Object* here reflects, or echoes, in its own way, a distinction of formal syntactical relation which must figure somehow in any account of those sentences given in any grammar of English. Thus such a grammar might distinguish between the subject (the indefinite singular subject) of the sentence on the one hand and its predicate on the other. Just what the formal differences are that mark this distinction of syntactical relation need not concern us overmuch. Let us observe simply that the subject is a noun-phrase and the predicate a verb-phrase, though the verb-phrase may include, of course, any traditional part of speech; and that the subject will normally precede the predicate, though inversion is possible.

When such a sentence is paraphrased in canonical notation, a transfiguration occurs. There is still a use, in speaking of the grammar of canonical notation, for the distinction of referential position and predicate-position. But referential position is wholly and exclusively occupied by the variables of quantification. The general term which in our ordinary English sentence occupied subject-position now finds itself, like that it was coupled with, in predicate-position; and there is no syntactic distinction explicitly recognized, in the grammar of this language, between one general term in predicate-position and another.

Does this mean that there is no significant semantico-logical basis for the distinction of formal syntactic relation we have just noted in our ordinary English sentences of the class we are concerned with—or, rather, for that distinction's working in just the way it does work in these sentences? If that were so, we might expect to find it a matter of indifference which of the two general terms available was formally fitted out for the subject-role in these sentences and which for the predicate-role. But, as we shall see more fully hereafter, it is not a matter of indifference. But if it is not a matter of indifference, then we have a question worth asking: viz. why, when two general terms, two non-identifying terms, are coupled in a sentence of the kind concerned, admitting of paraphrase into canonical notation in a way which puts them on a syntactical level as predicate-phrases—*why*, in ordinary English, is one of them rather than the other formally fitted out for subject-position, and the other for predicate-position?

I shall answer the question by invoking the concept of degree of identificatory force. I shall say that in any singular sentence of the class we are concerned with, in which two terms are coupled, one in subject- and one in predicate-position, the term apt for subject-position is, other things being equal, the term with the greater identificatory force.

With this notion of identificatory force we reach out beyond the class of sentences we are immediately concerned with, and connect them with sentences more akin to those that figure in our earlier and more restricted language-types. For order of identificatory force is to be so understood that an individually identifying term has greater identificatory force than any kind-identifying or non-identifying term; and any kind-identifying term has greater identificatory force than a non-identifying term; and some non-identifying terms have greater identificatory force than others. Any definite singular term counts as individually identifying; any sortal as kind-identifying; any term which is neither individually nor kind-identifying as non-identifying. Clearly the thesis is incompletely stated until more has been said about non-identifying terms.

Let us leave this aside for a moment and apply the thesis first to the easy cases in the problem area. In describing the disorder of a room, I might use some or all of the following sentences:

A chair was overturned
A bottle was lying on the floor
A picture was broken.

For the assigning of positions—subject-position or predicate-position—the grammatical criteria of grammatical category—noun-phrase versus participle in these cases—and of phrase-order are in harmony. If we reverse phrase-order—'Lying on the floor was a bottle'—grammatical category carries the day. Further, the result given by the grammatical criteria is in obvious harmony with the result which follows from the proposed general thesis: the terms favoured by grammar for subject-position are kind-identifying terms, the terms favoured by grammar for predicate-position are neither kind-identifying nor individually identifying terms.

Suppose, now, we try to enlist grammar *against* the result which follows from the general thesis by simultaneously reversing phrase-order and fitting out the expressions which the general thesis casts for predicate-position as noun-phrases. Thus we might get:

An overturned thing ⎫
Something overturned ⎬ was a chair
A thing lying on the floor was a bottle
A broken thing was a picture.

Obviously these are not equally natural and acceptable ways of saying just what the original set of sentences could be naturally used to say. Yet if there are no semantical or functional distinctions corresponding to the difference of subject- and predicate-position in our problem area—no such distinctions as the general thesis proposes—then nothing unacceptable should result from an attempt to fulfil the merely grammatical requirements for a swop of positions. It will not do to say that the unacceptability of the second set of sentences is simply due to their being lengthier and more cumbersome. Language-users in general do not find this a deterrent. Nor will it do to say merely that the unnaturalness of the result is due to the fact that of the competing terms in each case one is a noun or substantive anyway, and remains so when the manœuvre is accomplished, whereas the other is not, but has to be fitted out with substantival form. For this should merely make us ask: is there no reason, then, why *these* terms have *this* character and the others do not? Is there no relevant functional or semantic distinction corresponding to the grammatical classification of parts of speech?

It should be noticed that I am not saying that the sentences of the second set could have *no* natural use. I am only saying that they are not acceptable alternative ways of saying just what the first set of sentences could be naturally used to say. Thus suppose we try to find a natural use for the sentence:

A thing lying on the floor was a bottle.

We might do it by imagining ourselves describing a situation in which someone first just notices (say, stumbles over) something lying on the floor and then identifies *it* (the thing lying on the floor, which he has just noticed) as a bottle. Then our sentence might report, as it were in a telescoped way, the thoughts, 'Something lying on the floor! Why, it's a bottle.' But then it contains, in its underlying history, a concealed definite singular term, or individually identifying expression—'it, the thing on the floor'—which, on our explanatory thesis, pushes 'a bottle' into predicate-position and thereby makes the phrase-order natural and acceptable.

Next consider some of the cases for which we seem to need an extension of the notion of greater identificatory force. Consider certain pairs of expressions the members of which cannot be said to be, as they stand, either kind-identifying or individually identifying. I have in mind such pairs as

'hard' and 'hit me on the head'
'round' and 'flashed by (just now)'.

The members of such a pair might obviously be coupled in a singular sentence of the class we are concerned with. Forgetting, if we can, the formal grammatical character of these expressions and thinking of the kind of sense they have, let us ask how, if our principles are right, we should expect the coupling arrangement to go. Now 'hard' and 'round' are words signifying *properties* which we might expect to be *characteristic* of things of certain *kinds*. But 'hit me on the head' and 'flashed by just now' could not sensibly be said to signify properties which could be expected to be characteristic of things of certain kinds. Being *capable* of hitting heads or flashing by might be such properties; but not actually doing so on a particular occasion—for that makes no sense. So though neither member of each pair is a kind-identifying term, there is a perfectly good sense in which the first member of each pair is more akin to a kind-identifying term than the second. The notion of being of a certain kind is closely linked to the notion of having certain standing properties, including dispositions to certain types of action or undergoing; but it is not linked in this way to the notion of entering into particular episodes or events. Thus if the sentence in which the two terms are coupled is one in which neither is fitted out as a *definite* singular term, then we should, on our principles, expect the first member of the pair, and not the second, to be the one which is naturally grammatically fitted up for singular term position. And this is what we find. That is, we find.

> Something hard hit me on the head
> A round thing flashed by
> Something round flashed by

as natural formations for this case, and we do not find

> Something which hit me on the head was hard   or
> A thing which flashed by just now was round

as natural variations of these. On the other hand, of course, since the notion of entering into a particular episode or event quite naturally generates individually-identifying terms, we shall not be at all surprised to find

> The thing which hit me on the head was hard   or
> The thing which flashed by was round,

where the verb-phrases form parts of individually-identifying terms, as natural formations in their own right.

As in previous cases, I am not claiming that we could not think of any circumstances at all in which the sentence

Something which hit me on the head was hard

might have a tolerably natural use. (It would be a useful exercise, pointing forward to later developments, to think of such circumstances.) I am claiming only that the sentence is not a correct or natural variant on either of the original formations.

For the cases of pairs of terms like

hard . . . hit me on the head
round . . . flashed by (just now)

neither member of each pair being kind-identifying or individually-identifying as it stands, we seem able, then, to answer the question why, if they are coupled in a sentence with no individually-identifying term in it, the first rather than the second should be fitted up, with the help, e.g., of the substantival 'something', for the subject-position or the position of indefinite singular term, as opposed to predicate-position. We are able to answer the question by a natural extension of the notion of greater identificatory force.

But now what of the cases where the expression 'something' or 'someone' figures *by itself* in singular term position, with no escorting adjective or adjectival clause? We have such sentences as

Something flashed by just now.
Something hit me on the head.
Someone has blundered.

'Someone' and 'something' here simply signal non-identification, and that is all they do. So they certainly cannot be held to have greater identificatory force in any sense than the predicate-expressions. But, then, these sentences differ from those previously considered in that they do not contain two terms, competing, as it were, for the identificatory position. Each contains just one term applied to an object which is otherwise simply signalled as unidentified. If we tried to fit that one term out for relatively identificatory position, there would be no term left to serve in predicative position. But we can, without paradox or difficulty, fill the relatively identificatory place with a non-term, i.e. with an expression which shows the place to be still *vacant*, with the signal of non-identification itself. And sometimes we do it more pompously with an explicit disclaimer: 'An unidentified object . . .', 'A person or persons unknown . . .'.

This little explanatory essay has, of course, its limitations. But so has its purpose. It is by no means intended to yield a full account of the distinction between subject and predicate in the surface grammar of singular English sentences. It is designed merely to supply indirect supporting evidence that we can sustain a distinction between substantiation and complementary general character specification when i.i. disappears from the scene. This it does, and more: it encourages us to view the general function of substantiation not so much as a genus with coordinate species, but rather as a general function with, as it were, grades of exemplification: the top grade being the case of i.i. substantiation, the bottom grade (the case of substantiation at the limit of attenuation) being the case just considered.

3. Modes of substantiation

So far I have discussed substantiation and substantiating language-types under quite a severe restriction: the restriction which follows from the fact that we have contemplated no variety of mode of non-i.i. substantiation, except in so far as such variety could be assigned to difference in semantic type of *g*-words involved. Contemplating such a variety of mode of course involves contemplating the enrichment of our broadened language types with new semantic elements—something we have so far avoided, treating non-i.i. substantiation, as opposed to i.i. substantiation, as, so to speak, the unmarked case.

We can introduce variety of mode by a quite minimal lifting of our restriction, stopping altogether short of all modes of pluralization or numeration. I illustrate what I mean by appeal to English forms again—to the differences between the forms 'a certain so-and-so', 'some so-and-so' and 'a so-and-so', where 'so-and-so' holds the gap for a sortal. The force of 'a certain so-and-so' is fairly obvious, and I shall not dwell on it. The difference between 'a so-and-so' and 'some so-and-so' is less obvious. Consider the following cases:

'A policeman has been shot'

'Some $\begin{cases} \text{general} \\ \text{cabinet minister} \\ \text{V.I.P.} \end{cases}$ has been shot'

'I've been stung by some insect'
'I've been stung by a wasp'
'I've been stung by some wasp'

'She has just been delivered of a boy'
'She has just been delivered of some boy'

Now what is the difference between the cases in which we use 'a' and the cases in which we use 'some'? My suggestion is that the choice of 'some' rather than 'a' embodies what might be called an acknowledgement or recognition of the fact that the identification supplied, though perhaps the best the speaker can do, might be regarded as inadequate to the circumstances of the case; and that the kind of identification which the choice of 'some' rather than 'a' indicates or suggests inability to provide (though perhaps sometimes accompanied by indifference to or unconcern about) may be either further kind-identification or individual-identification. If this is on the right lines, it would explain some facts about my examples. Thus there is more likely in general to be an individual identification question asked in the case of a cabinet minister (general, V.I.P.) than in the case of a policeman; and more point, therefore, in acknowledging the question, as it were, even while disclaiming the ability to answer it. In my next group of three examples, the most satisfactory description of an unsatisfactory situation is given by 'I've been stung by a wasp'. That gives all the identification we need of what stung me. 'I've been stung by some insect' acknowledges that the kind-identification given falls short of what we generally regard as desirable in such cases (from the point of view, for example, of treatment), even though it may be spoken in a spirit of manly indifference to such concern. 'I've been stung by some wasp', on the other hand, with its suggestion of a possible individual-identification of the wasp in question, seems absurd. Even more absurd is the suggestion of a possible individual-identification in the case of 'She has just been delivered of some boy'. It is not totally absurd, any more than the question, 'Who is the boy she has just been delivered of?' is totally absurd; but it would require an elaborate setting[4] to be given any natural use at all.

Let us now consider briefly questions of pluralization and numeration. If we consider these notions in a quite general way in relation to some sentences of our broadened language-types, it seems theoretically possible that they might have been introduced in a less definite way than we naturally think of. Suppose we have non-i.i. substantiation +

[4] Cf. A. Trollope, *Is He Popenjoy?*, London, Oxford Univ. Press, 1944.

verbal general character specification + situational space–time indication. For example, we might have a combination representable by: man + dive + there past. We might now imagine a situation-pluralization-indicator, operating on the whole sentence, which was indefinite as between various possibilities: e.g. several men diving once each, several men diving several times, one man diving several times. This is more indefiniteness than we normally want or need. We could reduce the indefiniteness by linking pluralization appropriately to functional parts of our sentence. So, *inter alia*, we have the way open to further varieties of mode of substantiation.

One device, I believe regularly used in some languages, for indicating pluralization is repetition of sentence-elements. This would allow for the differentiation above remarked on; but if it were the only device available, it would be rather inflexible. If we were content merely to indicate pluralization, it would serve. It would serve also for a vague indication of degrees of multiplicity, for we could have one or more repetitions. It could even serve, up to a point, for strict numeration: but if we used it for this purpose exclusively, we should lose the possibility of indefinite pluralization and also suffer severely in the matter of economy. If we want to be variously specific about pluralization, we should do better to introduce a variety of semantic elements; again differentiating, as previously remarked, by minor linkage indication, the case when such an element is to be taken with substantiation from the case when it is to be taken only with verbal general character specification.

Some of the varieties of pluralization recognized in languages we know and which we may suppose introduced into our language-types include: bare pluralization; various vague degrees of pluralization (as: a few, some, several, many, a lot; a few times, many times, several times, frequently, often, a lot); and numeration (two, three, twice, thrice, etc.).

Now on the side of substantiation there appears the possibility of pluralized analogues for individually identifying substantiation. Thus we may introduce a way of marking 'Plural + man' to indicate that we are specifying or *identifying* some *particular set or group* of men. The deictic distinguishers already available for i.i. substantiation offer themselves for this purpose: so we may have a minor linkage of, say, 't + Plural + man' (cf. 'the men', 'these/those men'). Further, to the power of indicating various degrees of plurality in connection with substance-type specification in general we can add the power of doing so in connection with an identified plurality of a substance-type. We can allow the minor linkage (t + Plural + man) itself to enter into minor linkage with some qualifying degree-of-plurality signifier with the force, now, of *several of*, *many of*, etc. Similarly with numeration. It would be hard to imagine a language which employed these notions in connection with that of a limited or identified plurality (closed class) and did not also employ those of majority and totality, i.e. of *most* and *all*. So let us add these interesting quantifiers to our list. Once added to the list in this connection, i.e. in connection with an identifyingly specified plurality or closed class, they offer themselves for wider employment, i.e. in connection with unrestricted substantiation in general. But one may reasonably guess at an order of conceptual priority here; i.e. that universal or majority quantification begins with a closed group and is then extended to an open class.

Two modes of substantiation which rate a special mention can now easily be slipped into place. One—a special case of pluralization—might be called that of conjunctive i.i. substantiation. In Part One I explained why, in a certain logical grammar, there is no place for 'Peter and Paul' as a compound logical-subject-expression. But a theorist of perspicuous grammar, without the logician's special concern, need not have any comparable objection to recognizing the function of conjunctive i.i. substantiation: nor, indeed, to recognizing a special case of non-i.i. substantiation, involving reference to a closed class of which the individual members are fully specified, i.e. a form of disjunctive substantiation. Where 'Both of Peter and Paul' is admitted, 'One of Peter and Paul' or 'Peter or Paul' should not be left out.

4. Further matters: existence; negation; scope

In all language-types so far considered any sentence specifies a substance-involving state of affairs or possible fact and is apt for the expression of a proposition to the effect that such a state of affairs or possible fact obtains. Within this general sentential role we distinguish the role or function of substantiation from that, or those, of specifying or indicating whatever else is specified or indicated in completing the specification of the state of affairs in question. Substantiation can be effected in a variety of modes: e.g. it can be identifying or non-identifying; it can be pluralized or not; it can be numerative or not; it can be compound or non-compound; it can be more or less attenuated. Variations as between these modes are not, of course, wholly independent of each other. In all our sentence-types there will be a sentence-part or parts to which the role of substantiation, in whatever combination of modes it is effected, can be assigned. The functions which complement substantiation in contributing to the overall sentential function will include some or all of (a) complementary general character specification, (b) time-indication, (c) location-indication. In all the language-types so far considered the last two are always utterance-dependent, i.e. have some element of deixis or token-reflexiveness in their performance; and we have recognized the case where there is no separate sentence-part at all which performs these two functions. In all cases in which the function of complementary general character specification is performed there is a sentence-part to which this function is assigned; and in the case where this function is performed by a verbal, we have admitted pluralized or numerative modes of it.

Before we contemplate extending our language-types beyond this substantiating framework, there are three not unconnected matters of some importance to be considered. They are the matter of existence; the matter of negation; and the matter of two-place predicates (g_2-words) and scope.

(1) *The matter of existence.* Languages of our broadened language-types, we have assumed, include devices for pluralizing quantification with such force as belongs to English 'some' or 'several' or 'many'. Such a device can combine with, say, the sortal 'man' to form an expression with the function of non-identifying pluralized substantiation which can then enter into major linkage with an adjectival, say 'white' to yield a sentence specifying a possible fact or state of affairs (viz., that some men are white). Or again, the substantiating expressions could include an indication of group-identification while remaining non-individually-identifying; yielding a sentence corresponding to English 'Some of the men are white'. Yet again, all the elements mentioned in either of these two cases could be combined in such a way that they jointly have the function of substantiation and are then available for use in major linkage with, say, deictic location-indication, to report, for example, the 'further vicinality' of some white men, or of some of the white men: as, in English, 'Some white men are there' or 'Some of the white men are there'.

Now there also exists in English, as in other languages, an important piece of apparatus for which we have made no provision in our language-types. I mean what we might call the apparatus of explicit bare existential claim—expressed, for example, by 'there are', where 'there' certainly does not have the force of further vicinal deixis. So, in English, besides 'Some men are white' and 'Some white men are there', we have

'There are some white men'. In the simplified grammar of standard logic the apparatus of explicit bare existential claim assumes great importance, is, indeed, in combination with the device of variables, a main instrument of that structural simplification which is one of its beauties. Yet in so far as we are concerned to work towards an understanding of structural features we find in natural languages, perhaps we should not be precipitate in introducing such a device into our language-types. We noticed earlier that the simplified grammar of logic had no guidance at all to give on that little problem of semantico-grammatical explanation which I tackled with the help of the notion of degrees of identificatory force.

I do not, then, propose to modify or add to the existing semantico-functional resources of our language-types in order to introduce such apparatus. It is worth mentioning that, for substantiating language-types like ours, we could approximate to the apparatus of bare existence-claim by pressing space–time indication towards the limit of non-specificity; but I shall not seek to exploit this thought.

(2) *The matter of negation.* I have not so far introduced negation in any form into any of our language-types. If they are to serve as any sort of model for the facts, this is clearly a deficiency that must be remedied. So let us introduce, first, sentence-negation. In Part One I explained how, and why, it is that in basic singular subject–predicate propositions, negation can always be taken equally well with the predicate, as forming a new negative predicate, while nothing similar holds for subject-terms; and how we can therefore recognize the function of predicate-negation as well as that a sentence-negation, while recognizing at the same time that, as regards this class of propositions, it makes no difference to semantic outcome which function we take to be performed, in the sense that the outcomes are logically equivalent. *Mutatis mutandis,* this result holds also for our language-types prior to their recent broadening by the introduction of non-i.i. substantiation. But as soon as we broaden the notion of substantiation beyond the case of individual particular specification, the situation changes. We now gain a great enrichment of semantic power by recognizing complementary general character nega-tion as a distinct function from sentence-negation. We can accommo-date such distinctions as that between English 'Not many of the men survived' and 'Many of the men did not survive'. So let us suppose, second, that we recognize this function too and adopt some means of distinguishing it from sentence-negation. I shall not discuss what means.

One incidental remark: if we look at English from the point of view here adopted, we shall not see a negative quantifier like 'No' or 'None' as on a par with other quantifiers like 'some' or 'many', i.e. we shall not see it as entering into non-identifying substantiating linkages. Rather, we shall see it as a mark of sentence-negation and call in aid whatever transformational machinery we need to account for its fusion with a nominal phrase. And this seems natural and unforced enough.

(3) *Finally, the matter of g_2-words and scope.* Sentences such as English 'Every girl loves a boy' or 'Most girls love one boy' are often given as examples of sentences which are syntactically ambiguous, their ambiguity being such as is easily displayed with the help of the established logic of quantification. Now since languages of our broadened language-type will include combinations of the form, say, '(Many $+ \alpha$) $+ g_2 + (a + \beta)$'—where the Greek letters stand for g_1-words—it might be thought that these sentences would be ambiguous in just this way; and hence that the ambiguity ought to be structurally representable as it does not seem to be in the account so far given. However, to think these sentences ambiguous would be to misunderstand the notion of non-i.i. substantiation. This kind of sentence, as it appears in languages of our language-types, with a three-part major linkage, is not ambiguous at all: we may take the quite unambiguous ordinary English sentence, 'Several men are beating up some policeman (boy)' as an illustrative model for our sentences.

The rejoinder to this answer might be that in that case languages of our language-types are not as rich as they might at first have been assumed to be. And this is correct; though the error lies in the assumption, and not in the language-types, which, of course, can be no more than their simple selves.

How could we make them richer in this respect? Well, languages of our language-types will already contain sentences corresponding, say, to English:

> Mary loves a boy
> Jane loves a boy
> Jill loves a boy

If the propositions expressed by these sentences are true, then Mary, Jane and Jill, though they do not necessarily have a boy in common, have something in common. And here is a motive for introducing a new kind of compound general-character-specifying expression (for a new kind of general character): an expression formed by the minor linkage of a g_2-word with, say, a sortal g_1-word marked for non-i.i. substantiation (and, in this case, for secondary rather than primary role in term-ordering). When we combine the new type of expression in two-part major linkage with a particular-specifying expression (i.e. an expression with the function of i.i. substantiation) as in

Mary + (love + (a + boy))

the result is logically equivalent to the three-part major linkage

Mary + love + (a + boy)

But when we take our new character-specifying expression in major linkage with an expression with the function of non-i.i substantiation, the equivalence with the result of the corresponding three-part major linkage does not generally hold. For example

(Most + girl) + (love + (a + boy))

is not equivalent to

(Most + girl) + love + (a + boy)

We should note the comparison here with the case of sentence-negation and predicate-negation.

This modest enrichment meets the modest complaint of poverty just mentioned (and, incidentally, generates the need for some device of variable grammar for distinguishing the members of such pairs of cases as that just instanced). But, of course, it is far from meeting all the demands we actually make on our languages in neighbouring areas to this—in particular all those cross-referring demands which quantification theory so elegantly satisfies. If we want a language-type such that languages of that type will meet these demands, then we must enrich the types we have by introducing individual variables or some equivalent, e.g., the various types of pronoun which do their job in natural languages. All I want to insist on is that this would be an enrichment. To put the point in terms of the *a priori* exercise I am sketching: we do not, if we make this further enriching move, have to jettison all the types of structure we have so far described. We can add to them: we do not have to throw them out. Similarly, I suggest that when it is a question of understanding the structures of actual languages, we do not have to read the idiom of quantification and variables back into structures in which it is not evidently present. The attempt to do so, indeed, might make it more, not less, difficult to understand what we have.

So much for these three matters. How do things now stand with what I announced as the dominant aim of the exercises of Part Two: that of casting light on the relations of two conceptions of subject and predicate, one closely allied to current logical notation, the other more nearly linked to the forms of a large group of natural languages? As regards the first conception, the notion of a subject is really that of an expression filling the role played by individual names in the sentences of a notation one degree less austere than Quine's canonical notation; less austere precisely in that it preserves a place for names and allows that place to be filled by them. Before the recent radical broadening of our language-types, which came with the admission of a variety of modes of substantiation, the grammatical role of subject in sentences of languages of our language-types was tied to that of individual substance-specification in major linkage with complementary general character specification or space–time indication or both; and though a mild variety of types of subject-expression was admitted, there was really no large divergence between the role of subject, so conceived, and that of individual name for individual particular. With the broadening exercise comes a change: individual substance-specification is but one mode, though a centrally important mode, of substantiation; the grammatical notion of subject keeps in step with the functional notion of substantiation, broadens as it broadens: we now have indefinite grammatical subjects and plural grammatical subjects; and a significant divergence has appeared between our two conceptions of a subject. One of the clearest marks of this divergence is to be found in the point made above about negation. If we take an affirmative subject–predicate sentence in the sense of that phrase which is closely allied to current logical notation, the result of negating the predicate will be equivalent to the result of negating the sentence as a whole. But if we take an affirmative subject–predicate sentence in our broadened substantiating sense of this phrase, this equivalence will no longer generally hold.

Strictly, I have not given myself the right to make these remarks: for I have not gone through all the stages of presenting a perspicuous grammar for a language of our enriched language-types, and so have not actually defined 'subject' and 'predicate' for such a language. Indeed I left these notions undefined, keeping certain options open, at the much earlier stage of introducing g_2-words. Nevertheless the above remarks stand secure. Whatever the exact defining procedure we were to follow at that earlier stage, we could hold it true then that only (though not perhaps all) sentence-parts with the function of i.i. particular-specification were subjects of sentences; and clearly we could copy that procedure, whatever it was, for our now enriched language-types, with the general function of substantiation in the place of that restricted form of it which is individually identifying substantiation.

5
The Generalization of the Subject

1. Derivative roles and derivative elements

All the sentences of languages of language-types so far considered have a certain basic character in common: they involve the combination of substantiation in some mode with complementary predication of some kind; and the notion of grammatical subject of a sentence has been connected with that of substantiating part of a sentence. I want now to consider the generalization of the notion of a subject beyond the function of substantiation; and this is to be the last major style of enrichment which I shall consider. But I want to come at this a little obliquely.

First, we need some preliminaries. It would be reasonable to expect, given a systematic presentation of a variable grammar for a language of our richest language-type to date, that we should be able to discriminate between the semantic elements of such a language in a certain respect which has hitherto played no very direct role in the exposition, though I have alluded to it from time to time. That is, we should be able to discriminate between elements not only in respect of

(a) the *semantic types* to which they belong

and

(b) the *functional roles* which they can play or enter into

but also in respect of

(c) the *formal differences* they exhibit (in, say, distribution and inflexion) in actual sentences of the language with a given variable grammar.

Descriptions of (a)- and (b)-type differences belong, of course, to essential grammar with no admixture of variable grammar. Descriptions of (c)-type differences belong to variable grammar. Differences of (c)-type are also the sort of differences which the rigorous modern grammarian (of, let us say, to be on the safe side, twenty years ago) relies, or relied, on in defining his syntactic classes of noun, adjective, verb etc. But of course the theorist of perspicuous grammar has a somewhat different view of (c)-type differences from that of our conventional grammarian, as I shall call him. For the theorist of perspicuous grammar the description of (c)-type differences forms part of a description of one possible way of realizing the essential grammar of a language of a certain language-type. So (c)-type differences stand for him in perspicuous connection with their semantico-functional basis. For our conventional grammarian, dealing with given as opposed to constructed languages, this is not in general so. The more rigorous he is, the less reliance he will place on 'intuitions' about the semantico-functional base of formal differences, and the more he will try to confine himself to a purely formal characterization of those differences; though it seems that such reliance is rarely complete.

Now let us suppose that for a given variable grammar of a language of our richest language-type to date, the theorist is able to distinguish, no doubt among others, three formal classes (i.e. three classes of elements distinguished on the basis of (c)-type differences) which are such that all nominals belong to one of them, all adjectivals to another and all verbals (including g_2-verbals) to the third; and such that, at least as far as nominals, adjectivals and verbals are concerned, there is no overlap of membership between the classes. This is quite a large assumption; and perhaps, as far as any maximally economical variable grammar for our language-types is concerned, a not very realistic one. Nevertheless let us make it. (We have not required that variable grammars, in our constructions, should be maximally economical). Then let us name the members of the first formal class, *as* belonging to that class, *nouns*; of the second, *as* belonging to that class, *adjectives*; and of the third, *as* belonging to that class, *verbs*.

Let us accompany, and support or simplify, this supposition with one retroactive assumption or correction regarding our so far considered language-types. This assumption is that g_1-*verbals*, like g_2-words in general, have so far been confined to the role of complementary general character specifications; i.e. they have not, in the specification of our language-types, been allowed to enter into substantiating linkages.

Finally, let us suppose that all subject-phrases (or substantiating sentence-parts) have formally distinguishing characteristics which we can appropriately register by calling them noun-phrases (or nominal phrases).

Let us now consider how, on the basis of these assumptions, we might enrich our language-types in new ways. We might, for example, introduce the idea of *new and derivative roles* for existing elements or combinations of elements; or we might introduce the slightly different idea of *new elements*, *derived* from existing elements. There seem to be a variety of cases, distinguishable perhaps in different ways. But by far the most important difference will be between cases which do not involve any departure from the basic character of the framework of all sentences hitherto considered—i.e. the combination of substantiation in some mode with complementary predication—and those which do involve such a departure. I shall begin, as I have already remarked, obliquely, by referring to some cases which do *not* involve any such departure. My main interest in them is to point the contrast with the more radical cases which *do* involve such a departure; though the less radical cases have an interest in themselves, and are doubtless of many different types. I mention a few possible types, freely drawing on ordinary English examples to do so.

(1) First is the case we might be tempted to describe as that of nominals (nouns) generating both verbs and new verbals. English examples are: ship, eye, head, elbow; as in

> The merchant ships the soldiers
> The boy eyes the girl
> The man heads the ball
> The policeman elbows the students

(2) Second I take the case we might describe as that of nominals (nouns) serving as subordinate qualifiers of other nominals (nouns). English examples: house dog, dog house, house guest, guest house, heart hospital, hospital heart, sheep dog, heart surgeon, etc.

(3) For the third type I refer to the assumption that in the language-

types so far presented verbals have been consistently limited to a predicative role, i.e. have not entered into subject-linkages. Then we might now introduce a case of verbals (verbs) generating adjectives or nouns (but not new adjectivals or verbals): i.e. the case illustrated by English participal expressions such as: the falling tree, a fallen tree, the fallen.

It is worth attending to each of these types of case a little more fully and then considering some likenesses and differences between them.

(1) The first type of case I described as that of nominals generating verbs and also as that of nominals generating verbals. Both descriptions seem justified. The emergent semantic items really do name activities as some primary verbals do. But the verbals now in question are generated, rather than primary, verbals; for the activities they name essentially involve substances (other than those of which they are activities) of certain types, and it is from the names of those substance-types that the activity-names are derived. Since primary verbals have the formal characteristic of being verbs and do not share this characteristic with nominals, the generated verbals can be marked as such and distinguished from their parent nominals by receiving the formal characteristics of verbs.

(2) The second type of case I described as that of nominals serving as subordinate qualifiers of other nominals. 'Subordinate' here has a strong sense, as is evident from the examples. The outcome of the linkage is no sort of logical product of the force of the two nominals, as might be said of such superficially similar examples as 'child wife' or 'hospital ship'. On the contrary, one nominal completely dominates the other in respect of substance-type specification, and it must be indicated (as it is in the English examples by word-order) which is thus dominant, because each may be a contender for the role.

(3) In the last case, having supposed that in the first presentation of the grammar verbals are confined to a predicative role and have, in the variable grammar, certain distinguishing formal characteristics (those of verbs), we now introduce these semantic elements in a new role—that of contributing to substantiation—and in their new role they take on the formal character of adjectives or nouns.

Now for some likenesses and differences between the cases. In the last case it seems clearly inappropriate to say that the development in question involves the introduction of new semantic items or elements, systematically linked to existing elements. We have not got new adjectivals and nominals, new names of further attributes or types of substance which essentially involve the activities or happenings which the verbal specifies. We have just the same semantic content applied with a functional difference: i.e. to contribute to substantiation instead of complementary predication.

This case contrasts sharply with the first. Here we really do have new semantic items, though systematically linked to old semantic elements. The new verbals indeed name activities essentially involving the substance-types marked by the original nominals; but they name *specific* activities involving those substances: e.g. to *ship* is to put on board, or to transport by, or to take employment in, a ship; to *head* is to hit, or propel, with the head. There is a striking example in *Hamlet*, where the hero generates a verbal, meaning *to smell*, from the nominal *nose*; but from the same nominal could be generated a different verbal, meaning *to rub with the nose*. These should be separately listed in a lexicon of derivative verbals.

What of the second class of cases: that of nominals used as subordinate qualifiers of other nominals? In one respect they are like our cases of verbals used as adjectives or nouns and unlike our cases of nominals generating verbals; for we should not say that 'house' meant something different in 'house guest' and 'house dog' or that 'heart' meant something different in 'heart hospital', 'heart surgeon' and the recent vulgarism, 'heart man'. It is not, then a case of nominal expressions in their new use naming some specific heart-involving or house-involving attribute. On the other hand, neither can we say, as in the case of verbals generating adjectives or nouns, that the semantic outcome of their new employment is to be understood solely in terms of the shift of syntactic function. For then we should be overlooking the fact that the semantic outcome of the linkages is not fully predictable on the strength of knowledge of the meaning of the subordinate nominal concerned, plus knowledge of the functional change signalled by the formal feature of positioning. We could go so far, on this basis, as to predict that a *house guest* is a guest who has something to do with, or some special relation to, a house or houses; or a *house dog* a dog which has something to do with, or some special relation to, a house or houses. But one could not predict that a house guest is one who *stays overnight* in a house or a house dog one whose function it is to *guard* the house. (Even when the semantic outcome *of the whole* can reasonably be said to be predictable, as in the case, perhaps, of 'heart surgeon', the prediction depends on more than knowledge of the subordinate nominal concerned, plus knowledge of the functional change signalized by positioning.) This feature, then, of specialized semantic force differentiates the case from that of a pure functional shift; while the fact that the specialized semantic force cannot be assigned to the nominal in its new qualifying role, but only to the linkage as a whole, differentiates the case in a quite general way from that of a nominal generating a verbal.

I must stress that I am not contending that the differences I have found among these three types of case are necessarily characteristic of all cases which might be assigned to these three types broadly understood. I have merely used examples from these three types to illustrate some general differences which can be found in this area of derivative roles and derivative elements.

2. The generalization of the subject

Now although enrichments of the kind just considered exhibit these differences, they have one feature in common which dwarfs these differences. That is, they involve no extensions of, or departures from, the most general structural-functional character of our language-types. It is still true of all our sentences that substantiation and complementary predication are the basic functions which make up the total sentential function of truth-valued specification of a situation-type or possible fact. All that we have done in the last section is to provide that semantic elements which operate primarily in one semantico-syntactic role or function may operate secondarily in others or may generate secondary semantic items which operate in others. We glanced at the question of formal arrangements to mark, and make possible, this extension. But, throughout, no extension or modification of the basic framework of substantiation and complementary predication was contemplated.

The next step is to break out of this framework with another major broadening of our language-type—a second generalization comparable with the generalization which took us from i.i. substantiation to substantiation in general. That generalization removed the restriction on subject-phrases to the function of i.i. substantiation by representing the latter as a special case of substantiation in general. The next step is to remove the restriction on subject-phrases to the function of substantiation by representing the latter as a special case of a more general function still—which we might provisionally name *subjection-in-general*.

To explain how this can be done, I must first recall the conception of subject and predicate developed in Part One—the 'logical' conception. In the exposition of this conception, as in the exposition of the 'substantiating' conception, I started with the case of a specified particular and a specified general character of particulars being presented as assigned to each other; which corresponds, in our present terminology, with the case of an expression with the function of i.i. substantiation and an expression with the function of complementary general character specification standing in major linkage with each other. I then drew attention to a certain asymmetry which particulars and general characters of particulars have relative to each other, in respect, as I put it, of the possession of incompatibility ranges and involvement ranges. General characters typically have such ranges in relation to particulars, particulars cannot have them in relation to general characters. For every general character there is another general character such that no particular can exemplify them both at once; but for no particular is there another particular such that there is no general character they can both exemplify. Again, for many a general character there is another general character such that any particular which exemplifies the first must exemplify the second or vice versa; but there is no pair of particulars so related that every general character the first exemplifies must be exemplified by the second or vice versa.

I then generalized this relative asymmetry condition beyond the starting case of particular and general character of particulars; and on the basis of this generalized logical asymmetry was able to give a general account of subject and predicate apt for any proposition of the form Fa, whatever the category of its subject. To adapt the account roughly to our present concerns: a sentence-part A and a sentence-part B are respectively logical subject and logical predicate of a sentence S if (1) A and B are in major linkage in S and (2) A specifies an item of type X and B specifies an item of type Y and (3) X-type items stand in the same asymmetrical relation to Y-type items as substances do to general characters of substances and (4) this logical analogy is marked in a formal way by the A-part having the form which the subjects of our basic subject–predicate sentences have, viz. the form of a noun or noun-phrase and the B-part having one or another of the forms which regularly complement a definite noun or noun-phrase to yield a sentence. Let us say that in such a sentence A has the role or function of *logical subjection* in relation to B and B has the role or function of *logical predication vis-à-vis* A.

As already remarked, this account of logical subjection (with attendant predication) and the account so far given of substantiation (with complementary general character specification) have something in common. Both may be regarded as starting from the same basic case: that of an expression with the function of individually identifying substantiation entering into major linkage with an expression with the function of general character specification. (The basic case is not in fact quite so narrowly conceived in Part One, which speaks of spatio–temporal particulars at large rather than solely of substantial particulars; but the restriction can be easily inserted, or imagined inserted, for the present purpose.) Both accounts then achieve a generalization or extension on this basis. But of course the generalizations go in different directions. Our theorist of perspicuous grammar presents i.i. substantiation as a special case of substantiation in general; and in so far as he can successfully do this, he is able also successfully to extend or generalize his notions of subject and predicate. His extension of these notions might be said to be *translogical*, in so far as he disregards, in his application of these notions, differences which our logician wishes to mark with them, but *intra-categorial*, in so far as they preserve the same categorial limitations as before. Our theorist of logic, on the other hand, presents i.i. substantiation as a special case of what I just now called logical subjection, including what might be called i.i. quasi-substantiation (i.e. the case where the identified individual is not a particular substance); and he on this basis is also able to generalize successfully *his* notions of subject and predicate. His extension of these notions might be said to be *intra-logical*, in so far as he preserves in the generalization those logical features of the basic case on which the generalization rests, but *trans-categorial*, in so far as the application of these notions no longer suffers from the categorial limitations of the basic case.

Now suppose the grammarian can successfully absorb the logician's trans-categorial generalization of the logical notion of subject and predicate in his own, grammatical notion, generalizing the latter too to include not only i.i. substantiation with associated predication, but also i.i. quasi-substantiation with associated predication. Then since he has, by hypothesis, successfully carried out his own trans-logical functional generalization at the basic, categorially limited level, there is no reason why he should not repeat that performance at the logically generalized, categorially unlimited level. If he successfully presents i.i. substantiation as a special case of substantiation in general, there is no reason why he should not present i.i. quasi-substantiation as a special case of quasi-substantiation in general; or logical subjection in general as a special case of grammatical subjection in general.

The only question, then, is whether the above supposition is justified, i.e. whether the grammarian can follow the logician in his trans-categorial step. But the ground on which our logician relies is surely sufficient also for our grammarian. The logician supplies an adequate description for his extended class of subject- and predicate-terms, a description which refers both to semantico-logical and to formal-grammatical features. He drops the restriction to substantiation (or to particular-specification) as a subject-requirement, while preserving the requirement of individual identification. The grammarian can follow him to the extent of accepting his account as a generalized description of *individually identifying subjection*, whether substantiating or not. But since he is also able to generalize in another dimension not open to the logician, he can drop not only the requirement of substantiation, but the requirement of individual identification as well. He can say: grammatical subjection-in-general stands to logical subjection as substantiation in general stands to i.i. substantiation. Our grammatical theorist's general description now incorporates, indeed, a reference to the logician's general description; but this is a source, not of weakness, but of strength.

We may represent the situation diagrammatically as follows:

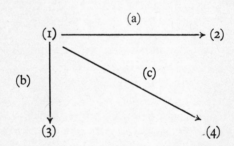

(1) i.i. substantiation + complementary predication
(2) substantiation in general + complementary predication
(3) logical subjection + logical predication
(4) grammatical subjection in general + complementary predication

(a) intra-categorial trans-logical generalization
(b) trans-categorial intra-logical generalization
(c) resultant generalization

The grammarian's generalization in two directions yields a resultant generalization represented by (4). The vertical component of the grammarian's resultant generalization is licensed by what licenses the logician's vertical move, the horizontal component by his not sharing the logician's concern with a certain style of perspicuous display of certain features of logical structure.

The generalizing proposal, as we have it so far, is quite abstract and brings, of itself, no enrichment of our language-types. It is nothing but a general form of proposal for the enrichment. It remains to consider the ways in which the form can be given content.

It is at this point that we invoke the notion of derived semantico-syntactic roles for existing semantic elements or combinations of such elements. If our general approach is right, we know what we should expect to find in any developed language for which this theoretical plan of development, or enrichment, supplies anything like a key to understanding—or partial understanding. We should expect, for example, to find *both* (i) derived non-substantiating nominal phrases which are individually identifying *and* (ii) associated non-substantiating nominal phrases which are not individually identifying but indefinite or variously quantified; though among these we may expect pluralized analogues of singular identifications. Further, we should expect non-substantiating nominal phrases of both kinds to be possible wherever the notion of logical subjection—i.e. of (3) above—can get a grip for the individually identifying case. And this is everywhere. There will be nothing at all that can be thought of which cannot in principle be 'presented' by a nominal phrase. For everything that can be thought of can be thought of as being thought of. So we may expect quite a variety of nominal phrases.

Let us look at a few of the varieties we find in English; note some differences in the ways in which our expectations are fulfilled; and raise one or two other questions about them. I shall select three such varieties and shall call them respectively (1) nominal phrases presenting universals; (2) nominal phrases presenting propositions or facts; (3) nominal phrases presenting non-substantial particulars.

(1) Some, though not, of course, all, members of class (1) are naturally seen as derived from substantial adjectivals, verbals or nominals. Thus, from adjectivals we have: *whiteness* (and *white*), *sincerity, freedom, bravery, roundness, fatness, wisdom, youth*; also *being sincere, to be sincere, being young, to be young*, etc.; from verbals: *smoking, running, dying, hope, expectation, hesitation, error, forgiveness*; also *to err, to forgive, to run, to die*, etc.; from nominals: *childhood, manhood*, also *being a man, to be a man*, etc. These are all individually identifying nominal phrases.

If we inquire what indefinite or variously quantified nominal phrases correspond to them in the way in which, say, 'a man' or 'some men' correspond to 'Peter', 'Paul', 'this man', 'that man', etc., we must answer by reference to such words as: virtues, qualities, colours, habits, characteristics, shapes, activities. Thus we have: *a virtue, some virtues*; *an activity, certain activities, some of his activities*, etc.

(2) There are a number of obvious and familiar nominal constructions in English for individual specification of propositions or facts. Among them are *that*-clauses, gerundial phrases and accusative and infinitive constructions: e.g. we know (expected) *that he left* (*that he would leave*) *early*; *his leaving early* (*his having left early*) was vouched for by the porter; we expected *him to leave early*. There are others less obviously having this character: e.g. *our freedom* is owed to *their vigilance*; *his firmness* is the only reason why we are still alive. The italicized noun-phrases are paraphrasable by other noun-phrases beginning with 'the fact that . . .'.

What of corresponding indefinite or variously quantified nominal phrases? What comes first to mind, perhaps, is a certain class of expressions which can figure both in individually identifying phrases of this kind and in corresponding indefinite or variously quantified forms: e.g. we have *the hope that . . ., the belief that . . ., the expectation that . . ., the assertion that . . .*, etc., as parts of phrases which individually specify propositions or facts, and we can also speak of *an expectation, a belief, a hope* and of *some hopes, many beliefs*, etc.

In using these nominal phrases, however, we do, in general, rather more than when we speak, specifyingly, of *the habit of* smoking, *the activity of* running, *the colour* blue, *the quality of* mercy, etc., or, non-specifyingly, of *several colours, many virtues*, etc. For when we *merely* specify a proposition by a nominal phrase, it is not thereby presented as hoped, believed, asserted or expected to be true. Rather *hope, fear, believe, expect*, etc., are primarily relational predicates that may be informatively attached to specified propositions and derivatively, by nominalization, yield such phrases as those I mentioned. It is only to the words 'fact' and 'proposition' themselves that the terms 'activity', 'quality', etc., are strictly comparable.

(3) Among the cases that most readily come to mind under the head of *nominal phrases presenting non-substantial particulars* are those of nouns derived from verbals and presenting actions, activities, events, processes, changes of a typically substance-involving kind: as, e.g., *smile, run, walk, laugh, flush, move, fall, kiss, death, birth, attack*, etc.

Now here, in connection with the relation between i.i. nominal phrases and indefinite or variously quantified nominal phrases, we have a very strongly marked contrast with the two categories just considered. In category (1) the singular non-articulated noun *names* the abstract entity; and it could not, without a shift in sense, be pluralized or given an indefinite article. We can indeed speak of *a hesitation* or *his hesitations*; but here we are quantifying over incidents of hesitation, not over abstract qualities. If we want to quantify over abstract qualities, we must move away from individual quality-names and have recourse, as remarked, to expressions like *qualities, characteristics, virtues, dispositions*, etc. In category (2), where specification of a proposition by means of a *that*-clause or a gerundial construction takes the place of the name of an abstract quality, the situation is similar. The difference I remarked on is that by a further nominalization derived, e.g., from g_2-expressions signifying propositional attitudes or speech-acts, we can present a specified proposition as a member of a class of e.g. things believed (or believed by X) or things asserted (or asserted by X); and the class-term, of course, lends itself to quantification.

In sharp contrast with all this, the nouns so far mentioned in our third category seem both central and indispensable for individual identification of non-substantial particulars and also immediately available for pluralization, indefinite quantification, etc. To that extent they resemble our original substance-sortals. And it seems that all nouns, however derived, which can be used to speak of particular *events* or *actions* exhibit this character. Thus we may speak of *a kindness, his kindnesses, many kindnesses*, etc., meaning particular acts of kindness. But it does not follow that wherever this general category of non-substantial particulars can be invoked, the nouns we use for items falling within it will exhibit this same feature of ready availability for pluralization, etc. For we might also say, of a dead man, that *his kindness* and *his intelligence* are no more and that the world is the poorer for their loss. What we here speak of are non-substantial (though substance-dependent) particulars also, particularized qualities, individually identified. But we are less ready for pluralization or indefinite quantification here. This does not mean that it is out of the question, only vastly less to the purpose than in the cases we began with.

It should be noticed—the point is implicit in some of my examples—that nominal phrases for non-substantial items of quite different types may have a common derivation and may often incorporate what is formally the same word. Thus we have *freedom* (or *liberty*) as the name of an abstract quality; we may have *our freedom* (*our liberty*) as standing for a fact (that we are free); we may have the same phrase as standing for a particular condition which may be at peril or cease to exist; we may even have the same word, admitting of pluralization, standing for particular distinguishable *freedoms* (rights, privileges). As noted above, *kindness* is another such case. Again, we may have *that laugh* designating an unrepeatable unique event; *his laugh*, designating something that can be heard again and again but is peculiar to him, though it may be exactly like his father's laugh, qualitatively indistinguishable from it; *his laugh* as designating something he might have in common with his father—they have *the same laugh*; and *laughter* as designating the quite general thing that may be heard in all climes and at any time.

New types of subjection call for new types of predication. But these also will often have a derivative character, though we may expect a new style or form of derivation here in many cases—some element of the stretched or analogical or even figurative, as the old substantial model works in the new forms. What underlies the ascent to non-substantial subjection is fundamentally the drive of reason towards second-order reflection and towards generalization, systematic connection, explanation; but we drag our materials up with us and have to adapt them as we go. There is a whole field of inquiry here; which I turn away from to raise another question.

That is: how exactly should we, as theorists, understand the relations between our nominalizations and the sources from which they derive? (And this is also to ask: how do we—as speakers—understand our nominalizations?)

I put the question in terms of nominalization and derivation; and this way of raising the question may seem to beg it against the latter of two alternatives offered at different times by Chomsky, concerning at least some members of our first category. It does not beg the question against the earlier alternative, offered in *Aspects of the Theory of Syntax*. There the answer is given in terms of the theory of transformations. Chomsky writes: '*Sincerity* would surely not be entered in the lexicon though *sincere* would. *Sincerity* is formed by a transformation. . . . It appears as a full NP noun-phrase . . . when the underlying sentence NP-is-sincere has an Unspecified Subject and the matrix sentence in which it is embedded has a non-Definite Article.'[1] But it seems[2] that

[1] Cambridge, Mass., M.I.T. Press, 1965, p. 186.
[2] John Locke Lectures in Oxford, 1969.

Chomsky no longer holds, or no longer holds for all cases, that such abstract nouns appear as the result of a nominalizing transformation. Rather, he suggests that there are underlying semantical or lexical elements which have no one primary syntactic role, but which are capable of appearing directly in 'deep structures' in either a nominal or an adjectival role. Neither form is to be viewed as *derived* in any sense in which the other is not.

Now the basic idea of this second alternative is one we have encountered before in these exercises: the idea of a semantic item, abstractly conceived, capable of appearing in different grammatical roles and exhibiting, perhaps, a formal variation corresponding to its role-variation. We encountered it, for example, in connection with the notion of a single semantic item signifying nearer vicinal deixis and another signifying farther vicinal deixis, each of which might appear either in the role of demonstrative adjective or in that of demonstrative adverb. Not only have we encountered the notion before, it may seem in one way peculiarly apt for the present case. For I spoke originally of *g*-words as words specifying general characters of particular continuants, capable of the dual semantico-syntactic functions of complementary general character specification and of being a contributory element in a minor linkage with the role of particular-specification; i.e. capable of functioning either as predicate or as subject-element. Why not, then, simply add the capacity to function as subject *tout court*? All we need is a grasp (a) of the particular semantic item concerned and (b) of the generalized notion of subjection. Whether a variation in actual word-form is involved is an unimportant and in any case a variable matter. We have, indeed, 'Sincerity is dangerous'; we have also 'Red means danger', 'Black is beautiful', 'Green is the colour of amorous passion'.

However, I do not think we should accept this. There is no reason to suppose that the two alternatives so far mentioned exhaust the possibilities. We may reasonably maintain a distinction between primary and secondary (or derivative) semantico-syntactic roles for elements or combinations of elements, even where we do not think it correct to frame our account of secondary roles in transformational terms; for it may still be right to view our general capacity to understand the playing of the derivative role as dependent on our general capacity to understand the playing of the primary role. If so, here is a justification for the (proleptically inserted) terms 'primary' and 'derivative'. And evidently my approach as a whole is far more consonant with the view that this is the situation with regard to the appearance of such a semantic item as *sincere* or *black* by itself in the logical subject role, designating the general quality concerned—i.e. with the view that the semantic item concerned here appears in a secondary or derivative role—than it is with the contrary view.

But I must add a caution against supposing that a solution we adopt for one case of a derivative form or role must also be right for a superficially similar case. I have already remarked that nominal phrases derived from the same source may nevertheless stand for items of very different types. Compare, for example, (1) 'Sincerity is dangerous' with (2) 'No one doubts John's sincerity' and the latter again with (3) 'John's sincerity is intermittent (*or* an unstable quantity)'. There is a marked contrast between the first case, where 'sincerity' denotes a general quality, and the second, where 'John's sincerity' rather denotes something of the fact-like or propositional order and where the case for supplying a transformational history which includes the propositional clause 'John is sincere' seems very strong. The third case, in which 'John's sincerity' denotes a particularized quality, is different again. That it is a derivative form is surely not in doubt. But whether we should class it with case (1), as non-transformationally derivative, or with case (2), as transformationally derived, is a question the answer to which must wait on a comprehensive theory of the derivation of nominal forms; and I have no such theory to offer.

It is not only at this point that my treatment of the questions I have raised under this heading of non-substantial nominal phrases is incomplete. My aim has been to indicate, rather than to answer, the sort of question that would have to be dealt with in any full treatment of the subject. I have already mentioned the question of new types of predication which must accompany our new types of subjection—a question which may open an illuminating perspective on the confused topic of categories. And I should finally point out that the three broad categories of non-substantiating nominal phrases which I began by distinguishing are far from exhaustive. I have said nothing about *institutional particulars* such as countries, nations, corporations; I have said nothing about *types*, such as sentences, flags, musical and literary compositions of all kinds; I have said nothing about numbers and mathematical entities generally; I have spoken of substance-dependent particulars of one or two types, but have said nothing of, for example, particular events of which the designation seems to carry no implicit substantial reference. It is true that if we stretch the notion of a universal sufficiently, some of the above might perhaps be brought under it. But this would serve only to emphasize another respect of incompleteness, viz. that within the broad categories mentioned I have been highly selective, making, for example, under the head of universals, no mention of *kinds* or *sorts* themselves as capable of being nominally designated.

3. The fitting in of features

I turn now to a question less ramifying and complex than any of these but nevertheless of some theoretical interest.

The foundation of the grammatical theory so far sketched is the notion of substantiation + complementary predication. And central to this notion is the distinction, among semantic types of *g*-words, between sortals on the one hand and non-sortal general-character-specifiers on the other. The former I called general nominals, dividing the latter into adjectivals and verbals. On this foundation we build with the essential help of the notion of generalized logical subjection and predication to yield generalized grammatical subjection and predication. Whence that enormous new range of nominal phrases with attendant predication at which we have just taken a cursory glance.

Now there is a certain class of semantic items which, it would seem, would be fairly basic in any language adequate to our experience, but which seem at first glance anomalous in relation to this scheme of development. They are those terms which are correlated with what I have elsewhere called *features* and which appear in what may be presumed to be their primary role (or at least *a* primary role) in *feature-placing* sentences.[3]

Language-types envisaged solely in the foundation-terms—i.e. in terms of substantiation + complementary predication—seem to have no obvious place for such expressions or for such sentences. Feature terms are neither sortals nor words for qualities of, or happenings involving, things which fall under sortals. It might be suggested that we could arrive at some feature-terms by way of adjectivals. We say of a thing that it is wooden or golden, using the adjectival in complementary predication; and the terms may contribute to substantiating linkages, as in 'the wooden idol', 'a golden cup'. The suggestion, however, is unhelpful; for it is clear that what we have here are *derived* adjectivals.

Let us consider more closely the nature of feature-words, beginning with those which stand for stuff: wool, blood, gold, water, wine, milk. How do they differ from and how resemble our paradigm substance-sortals and adjectivals? They differ from sortals in not, as Quine puts

[3] See *Individuals*, Chapters 6 and 7.

it, dividing their reference; or, as it is sometimes also put, they are not concepts which incorporate an arithmetic of their application, any more than such terms as 'red' and 'heavy' do. Yet they may be felt to be far closer to substance-sortals than to terms specifying characters or undergoings of primary substances. The fundamental point of resemblance is hard to express. Perhaps we may put it so: they cover the whole being of what they apply to in the way that primary substance-sortals also do and in a way in which character- or undergoing-specifying terms do not. Each stuff-feature-term means: *matter* of a certain sort, just as each primary substance-term means: a *material individual* of a certain sort. Terms for identifiable and countable material individuals are readily composed out of stuff-feature-terms by a recognizable kind of conceptual supplementation: *nugget* of gold, *bundle* of wool, etc. Even stopping short of this individual-composition, we find another powerful analogy or parallel with primary sortals: the parallel between number and quantity. The expressions 'some', 'more', 'a lot of' have all a double employment which makes this point with admirable force. Compare 'some horses', 'more horses', 'a lot of horses' with 'some gold', 'more gold', 'a lot of gold'. We can paraphrase the first with: 'a number of horses', 'a larger number of horses', 'a large number of horses'; the second with: 'a quantity of gold', 'a larger quantity of gold', 'a large quantity of gold'. Again, without any sense of incompleteness, we may sometimes simply say 'This gold is mine', 'That gold is yours' and make our references just as clear as when we say 'This horse is mine, that horse is yours'.

Even at the foundation-level, then, we may expect stuff-feature terms and stuff-feature sentences to present no very strong resistance to assimilation in our substantiating grammar. What we have to do is to find models in our existing framework for the sentence-types we wish to assimilate and then broaden the conception of substantiation sufficiently to bring the new and the old sentences under a common head. This will involve explicitly recognizing a new type of nominal and, as we shall see in a moment, introducing quantity-analogues of the pluralizing quantifiers. For our models we draw on both sentences involving i.i. substantiation and sentences involving non-i.i. substantiation as so far conceived. Thus a sentence corresponding to English 'This water is brackish' we assimilate to a sentence corresponding to English 'This man is bald', representing the structure of the former by

(This + water) + brackish

as we represent that of the latter by

$$(\text{This} + \text{man}) + \text{bald}.$$

As for feature-placing sentences proper, we find a model for them in pluralized non-i.i. substantiation, making use of the quantity-analogues of the pluralizing quantifiers referred to above. Thus sentences corresponding to English 'There is gold here' or 'There is some (much) gold here' find their model in sentences corresponding to English 'Men are here' or 'Some (many) men are here', the structure

$$(\text{Some }_{qu} + \text{gold}) + \text{here}$$

finding its parallel in the structure

$$(\text{Some }_{pl} + \text{man}) + \text{here}.$$

And so our original feature-placing sentences take their place within the general class of sentences involving non-i.i. substantiation. But we must not lose sight of the fact that the reason why it may be natural to proceed in this way—at least for a given language or group of languages—may consist in the dominance, in that language-group and its grammars of the notion of substantiation as originally and more restrictedly conceived.

What, now, of the ascent to generalized subjection and predication? This presents no problem. The feature-names themselves are immediately available as the names of *kinds* or *types* of stuff, abstractly conceived. How we classify what we regard the abstract name as derived *from* is the question we have been concerned with; and that question is settled at the foundation-level. Thus we regard the 'gold' of 'Gold is beautiful', the 'snow' of 'Snow is white', as derived from the 'gold' of 'There is (some) gold here', from the 'snow' of 'This snow is dirty', just as we regard 'manhood' or 'mankind' or 'Man' as derived from the sortal 'man'. The basic move is the assimilation of stuff-feature terms to substance-sortals.

Not all features are stuff. What of rain and cold? One of the relevant feature-terms has an evident affinity with the *adjectival* 'cold'; and the other seems to have a general affinity with verbals in so far as something happens when it rains. Yet the invocation of these features in a feature-placing sentence does not really lend itself to functional assimilation in a substantiating framework. What we get, in familiar languages, is a purely *formal* assimilation, marked in some languages by the supplying of the dummy subject, the non-referential 'it', preceding the verb or adjectival phrase. But this also is a kind of assimilation.

So features can be fitted into a basically substantiating subject–predicate language.

4. Further questions

In conclusion I mention some aspects of the traditional grammatical theory of subject and predicate which I have not dealt with at all in these chapters, or at most have barely alluded to.

I have loosely associated the notion of a grammatical subject with the function of grammatical subjection-in-general, a function characterized in terms of a two-dimensional generalization of our basic case of particular substance specification. Evidently many sentences will contain more than one sentence-part with this general function. But traditionally the division of a sentence or clause into subject and predicate is an exhaustive binary division: each sentence or clause has one subject and one predicate. So clearly some account is called for of the principles which determine the selection of one sentence-part, having our general function, as subject of a sentence or clause and the relegation of other sentence-parts, also having that function, to a place in the predicate: they may find a place there as, for example, 'object' of the verb or as included in an adverbial phrase of one kind or another. To deal with these questions we need further development along at least two lines I have earlier alluded to. First, in discussing non-symmetrical two-place relations I drew a distinction between primary and secondary terms; and, as far as these cases go, it seems clear that the notion of primacy is built into that of grammatical subject. More must be said, doubtless, about relations in the present connection; but here is one way at least in which the notion of a grammatical subject can be stiffened with a functional base I have not so far associated with it. The other line of development I touched on in connection with situational space–time indication, discussing why, in a binary presentation, expressions with this function should be 'taken with' one sentence-part rather than another; and it is clear that space–time indication might include a substantiating or quasi-substantiating phrase. But again it is clear also that the topic is broader than this. What is needed is a general account of why we count as adverbial all those phrases or clauses which we do so count.

What these two lines of theoretical development have in common— and there are yet other relevant necessary developments which would surely share this feature—is that they seek to explain the further grammatical restriction on the notion of subject (and the correlative extension of the notion of predicate) in terms of 'semantico-functional' distinctions and considerations. There is another aspect of the matter which should also receive attention, but which some might wish to assign to a different domain from that of the 'semantico-functional', perhaps to that of 'illocutionary force'. It is one which linguists indicate when, in connection with subject and predicate, they introduce the distinction of *topic* and *comment*. There are, perhaps, various possible ways of elucidating this not very clear distinction: one useful technique is to think of possible questions which sentences might serve as answers to. In so far as there are formal devices by which this distinction may be marked in the structure of a sentence: and in so far as these devices systematically overlap with other functional-cum-formal features of the subject–predicate distinction; so far will this distinction too be relevant to a full account of the grammatical notion.

Index

'a', 110–11
accusative and infinitive, 130
active, 89, 92
adjectivals, 103–4, 121, 123, 129, 135, 137
adjectives, 103, 121, 123
adverbial phrases, 138
adverbs, deictic, 95
ambiguity, 40
    syntactic, 76, 85, 116–17
article, definite, 43, 82
'assignment', 25–6, 29–31, 32–4, 80–1
asymmetry (of particulars and concepts), 18ff., 126
atomic propositions, see propositions
attitudes, propositional, 131
attribute, 32–4

Berkeley, G., 14
borderline cases, 18

categories, 25, 80, 134
category-absurdity, 81–2
characters, general, 80ff., 126; see also 'general character specification'
Chomsky, N., 132–3
circle, name-using, 42ff., 57
classes, syntactic, 81, 121
collection, principles of, 17, 23

combination, propositional, 21, 25–6, 29–31, 32–4, 40
    semantically functional, 77ff., 80
command of names, see names
comment, 139
commitment, 33, 38, 64
complementary concepts, see concepts
    'general character specification', see 'general character specification'
composition of predicates, see predicates
concept-specification, 21ff.
concepts
    complementary, 24–6
    conjunctive, 26–7
    disjunctive, 27
    general, 14ff., 37, 39–40
converses, semantic, 88ff.
Correspondence Theory of Truth, see truth

'deep structures', 133
deictic
    adverbs, see adverbs
    distinguishers, see distinguishers
deixis, 95, 133
    bare contextual, 82
derived elements, see elements
    roles, see roles

descriptions, 42ff.
  definite, 61–6
  identifying, 45, 47
descriptive names, *see* names
differentiation
  of concepts, 17–19, 27
  of particulars, 17–19, 27
direction of a relation, 87, 92–3
distinguishers
  deictic, 82, 97, 112–13
  indexical, 82
  interlocutor, 82
  vicinal, 82, 97, 133
distribution, 121

elements
  derived, 122–4
  semantically significant, 76–9,
    80
empiricism, 14
English, 8, 11, 29, 96, 104–10,
    122, 129
enrichment, 77
exemplification, concept of, 22, 26
existence, 114–15
experience, 14ff.

falsity, *see* truth
feature-placing sentences, 135,
    137
features, 135–8
fictional names, *see* names
force, identificatory, 105–9
Frege, G., 21
functions, semantico-syntactic,
    77–8, 84, 133; *see also* roles

g-words, 80ff., 102–4, 133
  g_1-words, 84, 103–4
  g_2-words, 84ff., 103, 116–17
Geach, P. T., 9n., 67n., 100
general
  names, *see* names
  propositions, *see* propositions
'general character specification',
    81ff., 96–8, 99ff., 110, 116–
    17, 126–7
gerundial phrases, 130–1

grammar, 10–11, 29–30, 72, 75–
    139 *passim*
  essential, 76–80, 91
  of logic, 41, 68, 75
  perspicuous, 75ff., 121, 127
  systematic presentation of, 76,
    93–4
  variable, 76–80, 82, 121
grammarian, conventional, 121
Grimm, R. H., 7n.

'hic', 97
Hume, D., 14
hybrids, 18

i-words, 80–1, 100
identification
  individual (i.i.), 101, 104, 110–
    11, 129–31; *see also* substan-
    tiation; terms
  kind-, 111; *see also* terms
identificatory force, *see* force
identifying
  descriptions, *see* descriptions
  knowledge, *see* knowledge
  reference, *see* reference
identity, 42
  names and, 51–6
  -statements, 51–6
illocutionary modes (force), 81,
    139
incompatibility, 19, 27, 34, 35–6,
    126
indexical distinguishers, *see*
    distinguishers
indication, propositional, 33,
    38–40
individuals (Russell), 5
inflection, 83, 84–5, 89, 93, 121
involvement, 20, 27, 34, 35–6,
    126

judgments, 14ff.

Kant, I., 14, 16
knowledge
  identifying, 47–8, 52, 54–6
  -maps, 54–6

'la', 82
language-types, 76ff.
  LT 1, 81–2
  LT 2, 82–4
  LT 3, 84–94
  specification of, 76ff., 82
'le', 82
Leibniz, G. W., 15
linkage, 81
  major, 83ff., 96–8, 99, 116–17
  minor, 83ff., 96, 112, 133

marker, separate syntactic, 86
metaphor, 82

names, 4, 12–13, 41–42 passim, 118
  and causality, 59n.
  command of, 47, 52, 56, 57–9
  condition for utility of, 42–6
  conditions of successful use of,
    46–8, 59
  descriptive, 61–6, 68
  elimination of, 48, 58
  in existential sentences, 60n.
  fictional, 57
  general, 43, 66–72, 80
  ideal, 57–8
  and identity, 51–6
  personal, 46–8, 81
  of places, 49–51
  primary (referential) use of,
    59ff.
  proper, 42–60, 62, 64, 68
  Russellian, 57
  variable, 60–1, 62, 64
negation, 6, 9n., 11, 24–5, 30–1,
  34, 38, 115–16, 117
'neighbouring' rule, 85, 89
nominal phrase, see noun-phrase
nominalization, 131, 132–4
nominals, 103–4, 121–4, 129
non-name-dependent (description), 47–8
non-particulars, 36
notation, canonical, 105, 118
noun, noun-phrase, 10–11, 29–31,
  32–4, 38, 103, 105ff., 121–4,
  126, 129–34, 135

numbers, registration, 50
numeration, 112–13

object
  causal or intentional, 88ff.
  of verb, 138
ontology, 95–6
origin, causal or intentional, 88ff.

particular-specification, 21ff.,
  81ff., 96–7, 100–1, 133
particulars (spatio-temporal), 16ff.,
  39, 41ff., 126–7
  complementary, etc., 28–9
  non-substantial, 130–2
  substantial, 80
parts of speech, 107
passive, 88, 89, 92
phrase-order, 83, 89, 106
place-indication, 95, 97
places, 42, 49–51
Platonism, 37
pluralization, 111–13, 129–32
positioning device
  major, 85
  minor, 86
predicate (grammatical), 81, 83,
  84, 93–4, 105, 109, 118, 138–
  139
predicate-phrase, 81, 83, 93
predicates (logical), predicate-
  terms, 3–40 passim, 75, 125–8
  composition of, 5–9, 24–9, 34,
    38
  conjunctive, 5–9, 26–7, 38
  disjunctive, 5–9, 27, 38
  negative, 5–9, 24–6, 30–1, 38,
    115
  restriction of, 4–5, 23
predication, 3–40 passim, 81, 132
  complementary, 120, 122, 125,
    128, 135
pronouns, 60–1, 62, 63, 82, 117
propositional
  combination, see combination
  indication, see indication
propositions
  atomic, 5

propositions—*continued*
  conditions of expression of, 58,
    61, 62, 64
  existential, 60n., 64, 114–15
  general, 67–72
  presented by noun-phrases,
    129–31

quantification, 3, 11–13, 32–4, 38,
  67, 117, 129–31
quantifiers, 102, 113, 116; *see also*
  quantification
quantity, 136–7
quasi-substantiation, 127
Quine, W. V., 3, 4, 11–13, 33,
  41, 48n., 67, 104n., 118, 135

Ramsey, 31
ranges, 17ff., 25
reference, 41–72 *passim*
  actual, 63
  identifying, 42ff., 82
  intended, 62–3
  theories of, 58
registration numbers, *see* numbers
relations, 84–93
  asymmetrical, 87
  essentially directed, 87–92
  non-symmetrical, 86ff.
  symmetrical, 84ff.
  syntactic, 76, 81
roles
  derived (secondary), 77, 122–4,
    129, 133–4
  semantico-syntactic, 84, 121
Russell, B., 5, 61, 65

scope, 116–17
selection restrictions, 81
semantically functional combination, *see* combination
semantico-syntactic
  functions, *see* functions
  roles, *see* roles
sense, 39–40
sentence
  -frames, 37–9
  -parts, major, 84, 96–7, 99

sentences, complete, 3ff., 37–8
singular terms, *see* terms
situation, distinguishing specification of, 95
situational space-time indication,
  see space-time indication
'some', 110–11
'someone', 109
'something', 109
sortals, 100, 103, 131, 135–7
space, 15ff.
  logical, 17–19
space-time indication, 95–7, 99,
  138
'stuff', 135–7
subject (grammatical), 81, 83, 84,
  93–4, 105, 109, 118–19, 138–
  139; *see also* subjection
subject (logical), subject-terms,
  3–72 *passim*, 75, 125–8; *see*
  also subjection
subject-phrase, 81, 83, 93
subjection, 125, 132
  grammatical, 127–8, 135, 137
  logical, 126–8, 127, 135
substance(s), 78, 80, 94, 101–3
  -involving situation, 99–102
substantiation, 100ff., 110ff., 120,
  122, 125, 135
  individually identifying (i.i.),
    100, 112, 125, 126–7, 136
  modes of, 110ff.
  non-i.i., 104, 110ff., 116–17,
    136–7
syntactic
  classes, *see* classes
  marker, *see* marker
  relations, *see* relations

t-words, 82ff.
tense, 95
term (of non-symmetrical relation)
  primary, 91–3, 138
  secondary, 91–3, 138
term-ordering, 87–93, 103,
  117
term-separating, 86–9, 103

terms
  individually identifying, 106–7
  kind-identifying, 106–9
  non-identifying, 105–9
  singular, 3–4, 67, 86–7
    definite, 106–8
    indefinite, 104–5
'that', 82
'this', 82, 97
time, 15ff.
  -indication, 95–6
  -slices, 96
topic, 139
transformation
  nominalizing, 132–4
  passive, 88–9
Trollope, A., 112n.

'true of', 9–11, 34–5
truth, 11, 14, 21, 22, 31, 64, 81
  Correspondence Theory of, 14
truth-value gaps, 58

universals, 5, 40, 129–30, 134
  of language, 78–80

variables (of quantification), 3, 11–13, 34, 60, 67, 115, 117
verb, verb-phrase, 10–11, 29–31, 32–4, 38, 95, 103, 105, 121–4
verbals, 103–4 121–4, 129, 130, 137

Wittgenstein, L., 65, 80